All About Dogs

All
About
Dogs

by

Jackie Marriott

Acknowledgements

My very grateful thanks to the following people for their contributions to this book:

Carol Baker, Nicola Barber, Bebe Bird, Andy Crumpton, Jean Foster, Pam Henderson, Angela Lee, Jan Lowrence, Diane Morgan, Alison Moss, Debbie Pe-ad, Sue Pope, Carol Ridge, Ann Rose, Stella Smith, Annette Standen, Rita and Harry Stockwell, Debs Wickham and Maria Williams.

Again, thanks to Sandy Enzerink BVMS MRCVS for checking the medical details.

Finally, a big thank you to Dr Tom Lonsdale for his suggestions on Chapter 6, Feeding Your Dog, and for helping me, and thousands of dog owners, in finding our way back to feeding our dogs properly and healthily.

Dedication

I feel it important to mention all of the dogs I have owned during my adult life, as each one, past and present, has taught me something new about understanding and caring for dogs. Owning and loving all of them has guided me through my dog training career. This book is therefore dedicated to:

Simon, Rupert, Brumas, Blick, Zilka, Tilly, Asta, Otto, Miggi, Beattie, Remus, Fliss and Kato

Contents

CHAPTER   PAGE

Introduction   9

1. How to Choose the Right Dog   13
2. Where to Buy   25
3. Selecting Your Puppy From the Litter   31
4. Preparing for the Arrival of Your Dog   37
5. Bringing the New Puppy or Dog Home   50
6. Feeding Your Dog   57
7. The First Few Weeks   71
8. Dogs Being Dogs!   91
9. Training   107
10. The Aggressive Dog   161
11. Neutering and Breeding   175
12. Keeping Your Dog Healthy   181
13. The Law and Your Dog   199
14. Caring for the Ageing Dog   204
15. Introducing a Second Dog Into the Home   207
16. Some of the More Popular Breeds   211
17. Breed Lists   243

Appendix – Useful Addresses   251
Index   253

Introduction

The decision to get a dog for the first time can sometimes be made without enough proper thought. What does having a dog within the family actually involve? I consider the first few months of having a puppy in the house to be more disrupting than having a new baby: with a baby you at least have nine months to get used to the idea, plus you have loads of back-up and advice both from family members and the health services.

Anyone can get a dog. You don't have to take a test and you don't have to know anything about his habits or instincts. Often, the decision to have a dog in the family is based simply on seeing one or two good examples of well-trained dogs, without having any idea of the hard work which has gone into getting those dogs to be so well-behaved. Perhaps you have recollections from childhood of the family dog who was your 'best pal' who accompanied the family everywhere. As a child you will not have been involved in the basic groundwork which resulted in the dog being such a good friend to you. You may have been impressed by examples shown on television of perfectly trained dogs competing in the Obedience Championships at Crufts, or seemingly telepathic collies working sheep. What you will not have seen is the hard work and time involved in getting those dogs to such a high standard of obedience. You may have no aspirations to compete with or show your dog, but the responsibility and effort in rearing and training a pet dog properly, resulting in a well-behaved family pet which is a pleasure to own, can be equally arduous.

The good news is that if *you* put the effort in, you too will end up having a new member of the family (albeit with four legs rather than two) who will be loyal, good company and non-judgmental. You will find that you make new friends, as dogs are great barrier-breakers. Exercising the dog will be good for you too; not only physically but mentally as well, giving you time out from the rigours of looking after the family or going to work.

This book is aimed at pointing out the possible pitfalls, making sure that you understand just what is involved in owning and being responsible for a dog, and helping that ownership to become a wonderful and lasting experience.

Why Train Dogs?

The relationship between man and dog goes back many centuries, when man discovered that dogs were more efficient hunters than himself. Over a period of time he domesticated them to help him hunt, in return providing shelter and a share of the kill. It was a partnership from which both benefited. This, combined with the dog's social needs, i.e. a pack formation requiring a leader (man), led to the forming of bonds which have lasted to the present day.

Over the centuries, dogs have been used for a variety of tasks apart from hunting. These include retrieving game, herding sheep and other livestock, guard duties, guiding blind people and, more recently, as ears for the deaf. Dogs that were good at certain jobs were used for breeding and as a result the distinctive breeds developed.

Nowadays, large numbers of dogs are kept purely as pets and do not have any specific duties, other than being a companion. Those dogs which were developed for working, however, need to use and develop their basic instincts. Training can either encourage this, or, where the instincts are undesirable, channel them into activities which are acceptable in society. Training is essential for the big, strong breeds, but is also beneficial for smaller breeds, to improve nervousness or subdue aggression.

Well-cared-for, healthy dogs are not carriers of disease nor are all dog lovers cranky or eccentric. However, because of the enormous amount of adverse criticism over recent years, owners need to train their dogs to be more socially acceptable. Nobody likes dirty streets or dogs roaming in packs in urban areas. Nobody likes to hear about sheep being worried by dogs, or dogs left out to fend for themselves. Dogs, unlike people, have no morals; they do not know and abide by our codes of behaviour unless trained and supervised by a responsible owner. We cannot blame the errant dog, any more than we could blame a cat for following its natural instincts and killing a mouse, or a fox for killing a rabbit.

The methods used for training are basically very simple. We make as much use as possible of the natural instincts. As previously mentioned, dogs are pack animals in the wild, one dog being pack leader. This is usually the most powerful and intelligent dog. He may be challenged from time to time by subordinates and, if a stronger dog wins the battle, the leader is replaced. In training dogs, we take over the role of pack leader, by inspiring respect and showing the dog we are superior to him.

1

How to Choose the Right Dog

The first and most important decision you have to make is what sort of dog you want. Do you want a pedigree or crossbreed? Large or small? Dog or bitch? Long-coated or short-coated? Puppy or adult? Here are some things to consider.

Pedigree v Crossbreed
Pedigree Dogs
Pedigree dogs are classified in two categories: Sporting and Non-Sporting. Within these categories are different groups, i.e. Sporting (Hounds, Gundogs and Terriers) and Non-Sporting (Utility, Working, Pastoral and Toys). Within these groups are certain breeds of dogs which have been bred to perform a particular task or tasks. A more understandable definition for the new owner would be to describe dogs as having been bred deliberately to herd (Pastoral), to guard (Working), to flush out game, retrieve and hunt (Gundogs), to dig and kill vermin (Terriers), or to sniff (Hounds). Sometimes these individual tasks are combined, so that you get a dog who has evolved into one that will hunt, point and retrieve, such as a Weimaraner or Pointer.

In addition to those traits already described, there are the dogs which humans in the past bred for use as almost a fashion accessory, such as the Dalmatian (Utility) – a very pretty dog which was used for trotting in-between the rear wheels of carriages carrying the 'gentry', back in the seventeenth and eighteenth centuries. There are also dogs which were bred to kill or fight other animals, such as Bulldogs and Staffordshire Bull Terriers. (A full list of pedigree dogs begins on page 243.)

What you must appreciate is that dogs bred for any specific role will still retain some of their original instincts, even when kept as a family pet. As an example, Border Collies (Pastoral group) have been bred to herd sheep and work outdoors for anything up to twelve or fourteen hours a day. They are extremely active dogs, fixed on their task and can seemingly run forever. They are, therefore, not the ideal dog to live in a small flat, or to be left on their own for long periods of time, with just a half-hour walk once a day! They *can* make good family dogs, provided they are properly trained and given plenty of interesting exercise, and preferably some form of 'work' to do, like obedience competitions or agility exercises. If left to their own devices, they will 'find' things to do to stimulate their brain – usually things that are completely undesirable in a family home! Left untrained, they will 'herd' other people and dogs whilst on walks, and sometimes attempt to round up cyclists, runners or, worst of all, cars.

If you decide on a pedigree dog, you will be able to obtain advance information from breeders and from books. You can be virtually certain of the size he will become (if you are getting a puppy). You will be able to see what kind of coat he should have. Each individual breed has particular characteristics, which you can ascertain in advance. You will be able to enquire as to what, if any, genetic defects the breed is predisposed towards. You will know roughly the life expectancy of the breed. Within each individual breed you can of course get variations of temperament. As an example, the generally perceived idea is that Labradors and Golden Retrievers make perfect family pets, and German Shepherd Dogs (Alsatians) and Rottweilers are usually aggressive and should not be considered in a home with children. Whilst not wanting to upset owners or breeders of any of these breeds, I have come across some Labradors and Retrievers who are extremely difficult and sometimes aggressive, and I have met several Rottweiler and German Shepherds who are big softies. The point I am making is that although the breed standard can be taken as a guide, the temperament of the parents of the puppy, the way he is reared, plus environmental factors, training and diet, all have an effect on the eventual temperament of an individual dog.

Crossbreeds

The term 'crossbreed' can in itself be bewildering. A first-cross dog is the result of a mating between two specific breeds, for example a Labrador and a Collie, becoming a Labrador/Collie cross. A second-cross dog is less easy to define. Some will say it is the result of a mating between a specific breed and a first-cross bred dog, like a Labrador and a Labrador/Collie cross. Others will say that a second-cross dog is the result of a mating between *two* first-cross bred dogs, Labrador/ Collie to Labrador/Collie. And so it continues – are you confused yet? The simplest definition is to accept that after several out-crosses, you end up with a Mongrel, i.e. a mixture of several breeds. That being the case, if you decide on a puppy, you will not necessarily know what size it will grow to, what type of coat it will have, and what character traits it will possess. However, devoted crossbred/mongrel owners will tell you how much hardier their dog is compared to a pedigree, which is generally true, because any of the physical weaknesses of the pedigree dogs originally involved in the cross-breeding tend to become 'diluted' as each out-cross is made. They will say that they are much more loving, less highly strung and tend to fit more easily into a family environment. Having myself owned crossbred dogs, mongrel dogs and pedigree dogs, I would say that it comes down to personal choice and that each type of dog is special in his own way.

What Size Dog?

Probably the first factor to be taken into account is your living accommodation and lifestyle. A large, active dog, such as a Retriever or German Shepherd, is not generally suited to life in a flat. Ideally, every dog should have access to a garden, but some smaller breeds can adapt well to life in the confines of a flat, provided of course that they are taken out several times a day. A few of the giant breeds, such as the Great Dane or Bernese Mountain Dog, can cope very well within a smaller house, as their activity ratio is much less than, say, a Spaniel or Collie.

Another factor to take into account is how long the dog will live. Generally speaking, the smaller breeds live much longer than the larger ones. Could you cope with only having your dog for seven or eight years, which is the lifespan of some large dogs? Alternatively, some smaller breeds live well into their teens – they may still be around when the children have left home.

If your family leads a very social lifestyle, it is far easier to take a smaller dog out for the day, in the car or on the bus or train. Visitors to the house may not be quite so daunted being met with something like a Cavalier King Charles Spaniel, compared to the visual and physical impact that an Irish Wolfhound makes. Even if your own children could cope with a large breed, could your children's friends, who will undoubtedly be visiting the house, cope with being met by a dog as tall as themselves?

Exercise

One very commonly held misconception is that smaller dogs require less exercise than bigger dogs. In fact, most of the smaller breeds can take as much, if not more, exercise than their bigger cousins. The larger breeds such as German Shepherds and Retrievers do need plenty of exercise – at least two good hour-long walks off the lead a day – but the Poodle, Spaniel or Terrier can be just as demanding. Giant breeds can require less, as they tend to be more Saloon car than Sports! Even then, they can still walk for several miles a day (when they are fully grown). Exercise is not just about tiring the dog out, either! It should be a stimulating and rewarding time for the dog, plus an excellent opportunity to help you to interact with the dog, aiding the bonding process.

Dog or Bitch?
From a purely practical viewpoint, males are easier to own as they don't come into season twice a year! Obviously, you can have a bitch spayed, which can cost anything from £50 to £150 depending on the size of the bitch and also what part of the country you live in, as veterinary costs vary considerably. Letting a female breed can be costly too, and should only be undertaken by the expert (see page 177). Most male dogs are easier to live with if you have them neutered (see page 176), and, contrary to one popularly held belief, it only improves their character, rather than changing it for the worse. Male dogs tend to urinate more often than bitches, and this can be mildly irritating when walking down the road, for example, with the dog cocking his leg on every lamppost or tree! Bitches will be smaller than dogs, which may be a factor in making up your mind as to which sex to choose. Very broadly speaking, it is my experience that bitches are more compliant than dogs, so for the first-time owner it may be best to choose a female. Although individual bitches can turn out to be aggressive, they are generally more passive than the males. On a personal level, I have found that the males tend to be slightly more 'devoted' to individual family members, which is very good for the ego of that particular person, but may not be ideal if you want a dog that will bond well with the whole family.

Puppy v Adult
Puppies
If you leave the children to decide, they will undoubtedly want a puppy! To a child, a puppy is cuddly, cute and fun. As it is the adults in the family who will have to do the feeding, training and clearing up after the puppy, then *they* must really want a puppy too. The advantage of getting a puppy is that, provided you have picked the right type of dog for you and have found out all you can about that particular breed or crossbreed, then you will at least have some knowledge of what to expect. You will also be starting on a clean slate with, hopefully, no learned behavioural problems or phobias to deal with. A puppy will also be easier to fit in within the family, as he will be growing up and learning with your children, and will not have any previous, possibly unpleasant, experience of children. It will also be easier for the puppy to integrate with any other pets you may have, such as cats or rabbits, for the same reason. The disadvantages of getting a puppy are that he will not be house-trained, you may have a few sleepless nights to contend with as the puppy settles in, they can be costly to rear, and you will have to teach him everything – puppies come as a blank canvas, and it is up to you to paint the picture!

Adult Dogs
Some people would opt for an adult dog, possibly from a rescue centre, for economic or sentimental reasons. There is a good case to be made for getting a rescue dog, in as much as that he needs a home, but you have to take great care that you know the real reasons why the dog needs to be re-homed. You cannot be certain of the dog's temperament in any given situation, most importantly how the dog will adapt to living with your children, if you have any. You may still encounter some of the same problems as you would with a puppy, but the positive side of having an adult dog is that he will probably already be house-trained, may already have

some basic training instilled, and will not involve the same rearing costs as with a puppy (see page 23).

Coat Type
All dogs, whether they have a short or long coat, will need regular grooming. Short-coated breeds will need a good brushing about twice a week, whereas the long-coated variety really need daily attention to prevent the coat from becoming matted or tangled. If your family routine does not allow for the time this will involve, then pick a short-coated dog. After a wet walk, the short coat takes much less time to dry – the long coat may need attention not only from a towel, but also from a hair drier. Some breeds will also require clipping by a professional groomer, and this of course adds considerably to the overall expense of keeping a dog. Irrespective of coat type, most breeds shed their hair continually, so regular attention with the brush and comb is essential.

Individual Home Environment
When it comes to choosing the type of dog suitable for your family, you need to take into account not only the size of your living accommodation, but also your family routine. If everyone is out of the house all day, it is not an ideal situation for any dog. Some people do manage, by having a family member or friend regularly drop in to visit and/or walk the dog. You could employ a professional dog walker, but this will add to the expense of keeping the dog (see *Overall Costs in Owning a Dog*, page 23). Remember that dogs are highly social animals, so spending most of their daily life alone is far from satisfactory, and will also make training and bonding much more difficult. All dogs have to learn to spend some time on their own, but this should be the lesser rather than the greater part of their lives.

Children
Children and dogs can form wonderful bonds which enhance the life of both the child and the dog. Having a

dog can teach the child about responsibility too, if he or she is given simple tasks involving caring for the dog – provided the child is properly supervised, of course. Children should NOT be given the responsibility of walking or training the dog. Even when held on a lead, dogs can be unpredictable on occasion, and, in the worst case scenario, the child could end up being harmed. If the children are still at the toddler stage, great care must be taken to ensure that the child and dog are never left alone unsupervised. Young babies especially should never be left alone with any dog. As far as the dog is concerned, babies make funny noises and smell very interesting, arousing his basic natural instincts and curiosity, which could have disastrous consequences. Having said that, don't immediately get rid of the dog if a new baby comes along. Just be sensible and vigilant and the two of them will happily co-exist. Young children can be unpredictable too, and can unintentionally provoke a dog into becoming aggressive. If you are unsure or worried about having a dog with young children, then it may be wiser, for you, to wait until the children are older, at least until they start school, before embarking on dog ownership.

Any children in the family **must** understand that the dog is *not* a toy, even though most dogs brought up with children are incredibly tolerant towards them and will put up with treatment that they would never accept from an adult. Provide the dog with a place of safety to which he can retreat when he's had enough. If all the children understand that when the dog takes himself off to his basket, for example, he is to be left alone, the dog will willingly put up with all kinds of things, as he knows he can escape whenever he wishes. Don't let the children torment or degrade the dog, however tolerant he may be. They must be taught to respect the dog, in the same way that the dog must respect them.

If you haven't any children at home, get the dog used to other people's children as soon as possible. Dogs who are nervous or aggressive towards children can be quite a handicap. Children can be quite unkind to dogs, prodding and poking them, shouting and rushing about, so make sure that the children to whom you introduce your dog have themselves been properly trained! At the first meeting, use food as an inducement and have the child give the dog a titbit, thereby giving a pleasant association to the dog in connection with children.

The Impact of a Dog in Your Home
If you are very house-proud, DON'T GET A DOG! Dogs will shed their coat continually and usually have two 'bumper moults' a year as well! Even daily use of the vacuum cleaner will still not remove every trace. Dog hair retains grease, and you will notice that all surfaces at dog height – corners of walls, doors, cupboards, etc. – will need cleaning regularly to remove the grease that is wiped on when the dog rubs past. Dogs get muddy – sometimes from just being in the garden – and guess where that mud ends up? Usually when you have just finished washing the floor or vacuuming! Dog hair sticks to clothes and furniture too. Dogs have 'accidents' indoors sometimes (particularly puppies). Can you cope with clearing up diarrhoea or vomit? Of course, you also have to be prepared to clean up after your dog has been to the toilet whilst on exercise.

Some dogs salivate profusely – Newfoundlands, Bloodhounds and St. Bernards are just some of the breeds which are particularly slobbery dogs – and that saliva can end up in the most unusual places! Dogs get fleas if not treated regularly with preparations from the vet. It doesn't take long for those fleas to take over your house. As well as these fleas living with you, they will bite you as well! Have I put anybody off yet? There's more to come! Puppies, and some older dogs, will chew anything and everything left on the floor. Clothes, toys, shoes, slippers may all be demolished if left lying about. Food left on worktops will be fair game to the agile dog. Crisps and sandwiches left on the coffee table will disappear! Furniture and carpets will be chewed if puppies are left unsupervised – some older dogs will chew too.

If after reading the above you're still determined to get a dog – GREAT. At least you won't be able to say that you weren't warned!

Holidays

When the family is planning their holiday, you obviously have to decide if the dog is going too. There are many places in Great Britain where dogs are positively welcomed but, if it is not possible to take the dog with you – perhaps you are going abroad to a country where the Pet Travel Scheme is not accepted – then you will have to make arrangements for the dog to be cared for whilst you are away. This could involve putting him in a boarding kennel, or arranging a house/dog sitter. Unless you can get a family member or friend to do this for you, either option will add considerably to the costs of your holiday. Either way, you will need to book the kennel or sitter well in advance. If you decide that boarding kennels are the right option for you, do go and visit several before booking, so that you can look around and ask questions. Even if the kennels are personally recommended, you should still visit them beforehand – perhaps they have had staff or management changes which may have altered the overall care on offer.

If you are going to be boarding your dog, it is a good idea to book the dog in for a short stay first, perhaps over a weekend, so that if there are going to be any problems, you will be at home to deal with them. Any little habits or phobias can be identified, so that when it comes to leaving the dog for a couple of weeks, the kennel staff will be aware of what to expect. This also acclimatises the dog to being confined and away from you for a short time, after which you come and collect him. When it is time for the longer period of being left in the kennels, the dog will have a remembered association with being left previously, and also that, after being left, you returned.

From a security aspect, if your dog either goes into kennels, or accompanies you on holiday, it is a good idea to put a temporary identity disc on the dog's collar with either the kennel address or your holiday home address. If the dog should stray from either, and only has your home address on, the finder of the dog will be unable to get in touch.

Overall Costs in Owning a Dog

Some of the cost of ownership will vary depending on the size and breed of dog you choose, simply because small dogs will eat less than big dogs, and pedigree dogs are not considered quite so hardy as crossbreeds so may need more veterinary attention. Puppies will cost more initially too, with the cost of purchase and so on. Also, as previously mentioned, veterinary fees can vary enormously from one part of the country to the other. It is impossible to give an exact figure of what your dog will cost you during his life, but to give you some idea, let's assume that your dog will live an average of twelve years, and that you are buying a medium-sized pedigree puppy, such as a Springer Spaniel.

Purchase Price: For a pedigree	Between £100 and £1,000
Initial Vaccination Course	£46
Annual Booster Vaccination: £32 per year × 12	£384
Worm Treatment: £24 per year × 12	£288
Flea Treatment (dog, house, car, bedding, etc.) £40 per year × 12	£480
Veterinary Insurance: Average £60 per year × 12	£720
Spaying Bitch	£137

Castrating Dog	£96
Food:	
Average £1 per day × 365 days × 12	£4,380
Identity Discs	£5
Microchipping	£20
Grooming Equipment (Brushes and Combs)	£20
Collars and Leads	£50
Bed and Bedding	£75
Toys: the sky's the limit, but initial toys approx.	£30

So far, and excluding the purchase price, your medium-sized dog will cost you £6,731 over twelve years, which averages out at approximately **£560 per year**. Then there are other variable costs, such as **boarding kennel fees**, which start at about **£10 per day**, **professional grooming costs**, starting at anything from **£30 every eight to ten weeks**, **dog training classes**, initial course approximately **£50**, **indoor kennel**, upwards from **£100**, **veterinary medical costs** – some conditions will not be covered by your insurance, and, even when they are, you will still have to pay the insurance excess of about **£50 per condition**, **accidental damage to furniture and carpets**, etc., this could be a very minor expense, or could be the replacement of your lounge carpet or three piece suite! So, make sure that you can afford all these expenses before you commit yourself to owning a dog.

2

Where to Buy

Having made all the choices and decisions about what type of dog to get, you now have yet another decision to make – where do you get him from?

Registered Breeders
You can obtain a list of registered breeders of the particular breed you want from The Kennel Club (see Appendix, page 252). They will send you a list of breeders in your area, but please be aware that this list will not necessarily mean that those breeders have puppies available at that moment. You may also see breeders advertising in the canine press or even sometimes in your local paper. Possibly the best way to get details of breeders, and also advice about the breed you have chosen, is to contact the Kennel Club and ask for the name and address of the secretary of the breed club for that breed. It is my experience that secretaries of such clubs are more than willing to offer advice, usually over the telephone, about their special breed, and will advise where a litter of puppies may be available. They are also usually very honest in pointing out the possible problems associated with their breed, as it is in the breed club's interest to ensure that their breed is properly represented and they know that all breeds have some faults, albeit maybe minor.

Some breeders are also prepared to sell adult dogs as well as puppies. They may have bred a litter and kept back one or two of the puppies from sale to see if they develop as suitable dogs for showing. In the trade this is called 'running on'. If the puppy does not then develop with sufficient potential for the show ring, the breeder will sell him on. Although there is nothing wrong with this practice in principle, you *may* end up with a dog of between six and twelve months old who has only known life in a kennel environment, who has not been socialised or had any training, and who is still living with his natural mother. The behavioural problems that this can bring may make you want to think again before going down that particular path.

You may also be offered a puppy on 'breeding terms'. Some financial reduction will be made for this, in exchange for your agreeing to allow the dog or bitch to be used for breeding. This could involve, with a bitch puppy, allowing the breeder to choose a stud dog and mate him to your bitch when old enough. The breeder may insist that the bitch returns to him for whelping (giving birth), and the breeder may also take one or all of the puppies for selling on, and may ask for all or some of the selling price of the puppies. If you take a male dog on breeding terms, depending on the arrangement, you may find that you are expected to entertain many bitches (and their owners), for several hours at a time whilst dog and bitch are mated, without any financial compensation or gain. Be it dog or bitch, these types of arrangements can be beset with problems, particularly for the inexperienced dog owner, and my advice would be to steer clear.

Do try and see more than one litter of puppies from more than one breeder before making your choice. Every breeder has his own thoughts on the right way to breed and raise a litter, so by making comparisons you should come up with the right choice of breeder *for you*.

Pet Shops/Pet Superstores
Many of these establishments are very well run, but generally speaking the puppies are litters which have been bought in. You will not be able to see the mother of the puppies, and neither will you have any knowledge

of how they have been raised. There is also the risk of
'impulse buying', or worse still, buying a puppy because
you feel sorry for it. My strong advice would be: don't
even go and look – you will have to be very hard-
hearted not to want to bring a puppy home with you!

Buying from a Friend or Member of the Family
This can often be a very satisfactory way of buying a
puppy, because you will probably know the mother of
the puppies and the environment into which the puppies
have been born. Of course, you will still need to ensure
that the parents of the puppies have been checked for
genetic defects, etc., and that the temperament of both
parents is as it should be.

Difficulties can occur with this type of purchase if
you discover a medical problem with the puppy shortly
after he arrives home with you. You may feel unable to
mention the matter, as you don't want to fall out with
your friend or relative. On the other hand, it may be that
you are *more* upset because they *are* friends/family and,
having taken issue with them, you end up falling out.
Either way may present you with a dilemma. If you
choose this route for obtaining your puppy, make sure
that you have all the necessary paperwork and information about the puppy, as you would expect from a
registered breeder. In other words, keep it as business-
like as possible.

Local Advertising
Most local newspapers have a pet column where you
will see puppies and sometimes adult dogs offered for
sale. The 'free sheet' type of newspaper particularly
seems to specialise in this type of advertising.
Although there is nothing intrinsically wrong in this,
some of the people advertising puppies may have little
or no experience in breeding, and may simply have
bred from their own pet bitch because they think it is
'good for her to have a litter' (see *Breeding*, page 177).
They may not have had the bitch checked for any

inherited genetic defects, nor may they have enquired too closely as to the temperament of the stud dog, or whether he had also had the required checks done.

If you see an older puppy or dog being advertised for sale, do make sure you know the real reasons behind the sale. It may be for a genuine reason, such as the owner moving abroad, or a marriage break-up, but not everyone is completely truthful, and it could be that you end up buying a problem dog.

It's not all doom and despondency though, and I have known some lovely puppies bought from newspaper adverts. Just be extremely careful and ask lots of questions. Once again, you should still get all the relevant paperwork and information, as you would expect from a registered breeder.

Puppy Farms

Sadly, puppy farming still exists and, although rarely sold directly from where they are bred, litters from puppy farms are often bought by retail outlets or advertised in the newspapers. Basically, puppy farms are places where several bitches are kept and used mainly as breeding machines, often having a litter twice a year, for several years running. Frequently, the bitches are first bred from when still immature, are bred from irrespective of temperament or genetic faults, and are not given the close attention that a bitch needs when rearing a litter. Because the bitch is bred from far too often, she will not be in the prime condition needed to rear a litter and consequently the puppies may not obtain all the nourishment from her necessary for healthy growth. The puppies are usually kept away from human contact and home environments, and are therefore not properly socialised or acclimatised to living with or being in the company of people. The result is that they are often very nervous or aggressive. There are always, of course, exceptions to every rule, but, in the main, puppies bred in such a way should be avoided.

Rescue Centres

Pedigree and crossbred adult dogs and puppies end up in rescue kennels for many reasons: frequently because not enough thought had been given by the previous owner before getting the dog; a pitfall that hopefully you will avoid by reading this book! Rescue centres are run very professionally these days, with great care given to the health and mental well-being of the dogs in their care. Obviously, spending days or weeks on end in a kennel is not good for any dog, and however hard the staff try, in a kennel environment it is not possible to reproduce the kind of attention that a dog will receive within a loving family home.

As much care as possible is taken in getting a full history from the previous owner when a dog is handed in – of course, sometimes people are not completely truthful, so the full reasons may never be known. With stray dogs, no previous history is available to the rescue centre, but, in all instances, the staff will do as much assessment as is possible while the dog is in their care to ensure that he is re-homed appropriately.

When a litter of puppies is either born at the centre, or brought in for whatever reason, it may not be obvious what breed of dog the puppies are. An educated guess is made by the staff, going on size, colouring and sometimes temperament of the puppies. All too frequently the litter is cross-bred, and often will end up being described as, for example, a Collie Cross. Given that within the Collie breed there are several different varieties, ranging from the small Shetland Sheepdog to the much bigger Rough Collie, and from the Border Collie to the Bearded Collie, it really is pot luck what you may end up with in the way of size and temperament.

If you decide that you would like to give a home to either a puppy or adult dog from a rescue organisation, be prepared for them to ask you lots of questions! As well as doing their best to match the right dog with the right family, they will also want to avoid the situation where a newly re-homed dog is returned after a few weeks because the family cannot cope. One of the biggest rescue kennels in the country takes in over ten thousand dogs per year. You can also expect to have a home check prior to being accepted, and also for them to refuse you if there are very young children at home. Most rescue centres also follow up on dogs which have been re-homed with an after-care visit. I know that some people can feel rather aggrieved at the questions and limitations imposed, but the centres would not be doing their job properly if they accepted everyone on face value. They have the task of re-homing a possibly already traumatised dog, and need to know that not only will it be properly and lovingly looked after, but that the potential new owners are prepared for the possible problems which may occur.

At my training club at least a third of the dogs which attend are from rescue centres, and I have seen many times how, with the proper care, a 'rescue' dog can be successfully integrated into a new home.

3

Selecting Your Puppy From the Litter

If you have decided on a puppy rather than an adult dog, have agreed which sex you are having and have chosen the breeder, the exciting moment will then arrive when you go to see the puppies for the first time. Don't be disappointed if the breeder wants you to wait until the puppies are about four weeks old – this is the best time to see them. Any earlier and it is difficult to tell them apart, and it is also stressful for both Mum and pups to have prospective buyers around, not to mention the risk of bringing infection into the litter. At four weeks, the pups will have eyes open, be well on the way to being weaned, and will look more like miniature versions of the adult dog. They will also be more active and less likely to sleep all the way through your visit! For the first visit the breeder may well ask that just the adults in the family come, again so that the bitch and her pups are not too stressed.

Bearing in mind that you cannot determine the sex of a bitch's unborn puppies, you may well not have a choice of puppy. If that is the case, then it is up to you whether you decide to take what is on offer, or wait for that particular breeder, or another of your choice, to breed another litter – always bearing in mind that the same thing could happen again.

Choosing Your Puppy
The size of the litter and ratio of dogs to bitches can play a part in the overall temperament of the litter. The absolute ideal would be six puppies, comprising three

dogs and three bitches. Size-wise, six would be easy for the mother to rear, and six puppies would have just enough competition for food and toys to allow them to develop as social animals. An even balance between the sexes often gives a more clearly defined difference in temperament between males and females. If a litter is predominantly male, for example, you may find that any bitches will have more of a masculine temperament. Likewise, a predominantly female litter with only one or two males may result in the males being of a softer temperament. This is not necessarily a bad thing, but simply something to be aware of.

Small litters, say two or three, or large litters of twelve, are not a bad sign, but could make your choice either more difficult, if there are several to choose from, or more restricted, if the litter is small. Occasionally, there may only be one puppy, often sadly caused by puppies being stillborn, or by illness wiping out most of the litter. A single puppy will undoubtedly get the very best nutrition from the bitch, as there will be no competition, so he or she will probably be big and healthy. From a temperament point of view, not having any siblings will mean that he may not learn to play or learn how to interact with other dogs, so he might be either a bit on the shy side, or could end up not liking other dogs. In my experience of owning an only puppy, my dog developed into a devoted family dog, who wasn't particularly concerned with interacting with other dogs or people, but who was not aggressive. I had to teach him how to play, which was quite difficult, but he learned eventually. I also know of other single puppies who have developed into the 'life and soul of the party', which only goes to show that a single puppy is not necessarily to be avoided, but may just need more careful thought as to how he is handled.

Before you even look at the puppies, try and have a good look at, and interact with, the mother of the puppies. You should already have ascertained how old the mother is. Ideally she should be at least two years of age, which gives her the chance to mature properly before being burdened with motherhood. If the bitch is under a year, she may well be too immature, both physically and mentally, to rear a litter well. It is quite usual for the bitch to be slightly apprehensive of you while her puppies are around, as she will obviously be protective of them, so try and arrange to see her first without the puppies. Although there are many factors which form a puppy's temperament, the pups will inherit many traits from *both* parents, and learn much from their mother whilst in the litter. It will often not be possible to see the father of the puppies, as frequently the owner of the bitch does not own the stud dog. Your assessment has therefore to be based on the temperament of the mother. If she is fearful of humans, the pups may well be too. If she is frightened of loud noises, the pups will pick that up from her. If she is calm and gentle, willing to socialise with you, she will pass that attitude on to her pups.

Ask the breeder whether the pups are being acclimatised to household noises, such as washing machines and vacuum cleaners. Have they been handled regularly? If the pups are kept outside the house, find out if they have ever been brought indoors. If the puppies are being kept isolated from normal household sights and sounds, you will have a harder job of settling the puppy you choose into your home environment.

Check the overall condition of both the litter and the mother. Are the eyes and noses clean? Is there any sneezing or coughing? Look at the puppies' coats. Are they clean and pleasant smelling? Is the area where they are being kept clean and free from stale urine and faeces?

Assuming you have a choice, picking *the one* for you is certainly not an exact science, but there are some general guidelines that are worth considering. Above everything, temperament *must* be the most important factor. Try not to be influenced by a 'pretty face'. Quite apart from anything else, frequently the best looking puppy does not grow into the best looking dog. Even if the puppy does turn out to be very good-looking, if the temperament doesn't match the looks, you could end up with problems.

Take into account your living arrangements and family routine. If your family is, for example, quite noisy, then you do not want to pick the quietest puppy in the litter – that puppy will do best in a calmer environment. Neither do you want the noisiest puppy in the litter if your home life is of a quiet nature. For first-time dog owners, I would certainly not recommend the biggest, pushiest puppy. That pup has developed his character by demanding his own way amongst his litter mates, and, possibly through sending out aggressive signals to his siblings, has gained first and best position at the 'milk bar', first choice of food on offer, and possession of the best toys. You can therefore expect him to try the same tactics with his new human family. Unless you are fairly experienced with dogs, you may be in for quite a rough ride with this type of puppy.

There are some simple tests that you can do to get an idea of the pup's temperament, but it would be courteous to explain first to the breeder what you intend doing. While sitting on the floor and cuddling the pup, *gently* turn the pup onto his back and place him on the floor, keeping him in place with very soft pressure. You can expect the pup to struggle for a few seconds, but he should then relax and be happy to lie there, while you gently stroke him, for at least ten seconds. This shows compliance, and indicates that the puppy will accept that you are in charge, making training that much easier. If the puppy continues to struggle throughout this procedure, it could be that this puppy will not adapt so well to being taught to lie down, or to stay.

Having played with the puppies, stand up, turn your back and walk away a few feet. See which puppy follows you immediately. Puppies that follow tend to be more sociable with humans, to enjoy human contact, and are unlikely to be shy of strangers. Similarly, throw the toys for the puppies and observe which is the quickest to chase. You want the pup to be interested in the toy, but the puppy who hangs on to it and won't allow the others to share is likely to grow up to be more possessive. This could show up later as aggressiveness with food, stealing and running off with things, or taking control of a chair and refusing to move.

Gently clap your hands and encourage the puppies to come to you. The puppy that hangs back and is reluctant to come to you may be very timid and unsure of coming to a stranger, *or* may be very independent and not feel the need to interact with humans. Either one does not bode well for a family dog. The puppy who gets to you first will probably be very sociable, so be prepared for that one to want to speak to everyone when out walking in the park. That isn't necessarily a fault, it is simply a case of whether that is acceptable to you. The puppy who appears to think for a few seconds and to assess the situation before approaching is possibly a better choice. This puppy will be friendly, but not 'over the top' with visitors.

When you have finally made your decision, if the puppies have identical markings you can expect the breeder to mark your chosen puppy in some way – sometimes they put a tiny spot of nail varnish on the tip of your chosen puppy's ear, sometimes they will cut a little fur off from somewhere on the puppy's body, and sometimes they will put a little coloured ribbon collar around your puppy's neck. It is a good idea for you to take several photographs of your puppy from various angles – puppies change rapidly, and the more means of identification you have the better.

Collecting the Puppy
Probably the next thing you will want to know from the breeder is *when* you can have your puppy. The first few weeks of a puppy's life are crucial to his eventual development. He is changing and learning daily. If the pup leaves his natural mother too early, some vital

socialising techniques will not have been learned. Up until seven weeks of age, the pup needs both Mum and siblings to continue the development of his inter-canine skills and he is still vulnerable. The ideal time for the pup to develop new bonds, and for transferring loyalty, is between seven and eight weeks. At this age the puppy is neurologically complete and able to learn, whilst still being physically unable to compete with adult dogs.

There are still some breeders who will not let their puppies leave until ten weeks or over. Puppies who stay with their natural mum and siblings beyond eight weeks frequently suffer from the lack of those vital two weeks of socialising with other humans and in other situations. As a result, they may end up shy or fearful, and have far more difficulty in adapting to their change of environment.

4

Preparing for the Arrival of Your Dog

Deciding on a Name

During the three to four weeks from selecting your puppy to bringing him home, you will need to make several decisions. The first is a choice of name. This is obviously a very personal thing, but there are still some things to bear in mind before you finally select your puppy's name.

Dogs can learn a variety of sounds which will become associated with various things, but the most important is his name sound. You will be using the puppy's name before every command you give him, and you therefore need to choose a sound that is easily picked up by the pup. Try to keep the name short, as a longer name is more difficult for the pup to isolate. As an example, 'Bilbo Baggins' may sound very amusing, but is extremely hard for the pup to pick up on. Try to choose a name with a clearly defined beginning and end, like 'Topsy', which gives a nice clear 'Toh' sound at the start and a 'See' sound at the end. Another example of a difficult sound for the dog to hear would be 'Anna' – a soft beginning and a soft ending. 'Fritz', on the other hand, has a hard 'Frr' at the beginning and a 'Tss' at the end, being an easier sound for the dog to isolate.

Most people try to be original in their choice of name for their dog, as they like to be different. Please don't try and be too different though – the pup may have so much difficulty learning it that in the end he just ignores it altogether!

Naming an Adult Dog

If you are getting an adult dog, he will already have a name. You may want to keep that name, but the dog can learn a new name sound if you decide that you don't like the original one. It is particularly worth considering changing the name if the dog has been previously ill-treated, as the name is a permanent connection in the mind of the dog with the perpetrator of that treatment. Try to use the same criteria as described for naming a puppy. Once you have decided on the new name, join it onto the end of the old name each time you speak to the dog. For example, if the dog is called Buster, and you want to change it to Ben, you would say 'BusterBen'. At first, place more emphasis on the 'Buster' part, and then slowly, over a couple of weeks, begin to emphasise the 'Ben' sound. After another couple of weeks, perhaps even sooner, you can drop the Buster altogether. Make sure that each time the dog is fed, or given a treat, the name is used – the dog will learn much quicker if food is involved!

What will the Dog or Puppy Sleep in?

Before you go and spend a considerable amount on a dog bed, give some thought to what puppies tend to do when they start teething – they CHEW. Adult dogs may well be feeling unsettled when they are re-homed, and this could prompt them into chewing too. If you have spent money on a lovely bed and bedding, you will be none too impressed if it is all destroyed within weeks! It is probably best to start off with a substantial cardboard box, having checked that it does not have any sharp staples or sticky tape still attached. Put a couple of blankets, or possibly a piece of veterinary bedding, in the box. Provided it is placed in a warm, draught-proof position, this will suffice as a perfectly acceptable bed until the puppy has passed through the chewing stage. Then you can go and get the 'state of the art' dog bed if you wish!

Where will the Bed be Placed?

Where the dog or puppy sleeps is often the source of many an argument, so try and get it sorted before you bring the dog home. Even dog experts can disagree about where the dog should sleep! Some people will say that the kitchen is the obvious place – it is usually one of the warmest rooms in the house, often the floor surface is more easily cleaned should there be any 'accidents', and there is no expensive furniture for the dog to chew (always assuming he doesn't start on the kitchen units!). During the daytime the kitchen tends to be the hub of family life and as such the puppy will be easy to supervise, even when in his bed.

Other experts will tell you that as the dog is a pack animal, the obvious place for him to sleep is with the head of the pack, i.e. you. If you allow the dog free run of the bedroom at night-time, I can virtually guarantee that you will have some sleepless nights in front of you!

My particular preference is for a slight compromise – I like to have my dogs in with me at night-time, because I do subscribe to the pack theory, but I do not feel happy about a puppy being able to roam about, possibly getting into danger by chewing electric wires and so on, while I am asleep (assuming I am able to sleep, that is!). I therefore put any puppy I have in an indoor kennel at bedtime.

Indoor Kennels – New Puppies

Get any thought of a huge wooden construction with an arched roof out of your head! An indoor kennel is constructed from rigid, welded, galvanised mesh, with four sides (one as a door), a floor and a roof. It provides a completely enclosed, see-through and safe den for your dog. I know that some people are initially horrified at the thought of confining their puppy within a steel 'cage'. I can promise you that your puppy will very quickly accept such confinement. Indeed, dogs are natural denning animals: if left to their own devices they will usually create their own dens around your

Fig. 1. An indoor kennel provides a completely enclosed, see-through and safe den for your dog.

home without your realising it. Under a table or chair, in a corner of the room – all these areas become a den for the dog.

The indoor kennel should be big enough for the dog to stand up, turn around and stretch. One end should house the dog's bed, and the other should contain a bowl of water (fixed to the side of the pen if possible). You can either make the kennel yourself, or purchase one from a specialist company, either through your pet shop or from suppliers who advertise in the dog press. The kennel should be made so that it completely folds flat, enabling you to move it around as you wish. For example, during the day the kennel can be in the kitchen, then moved to the bedroom at night.

Indoor kennels have a couple of very definite advantages. It is rare for a puppy to soil his own sleeping area, so the indoor kennel is a very positive aid in house-training your puppy. Of course, the puppy must first be allowed access to his toilet area before being put in the kennel and you can expect some very early morning starts for the first few weeks! The other huge advantage of acclimatising a puppy to regular periods of confinement is that when the puppy has to be left alone for an hour or so during the day, you can put him into his kennel and he will not have access to the areas he is likely to want to **chew!** Make sure that during these periods he has one or two safe, sensible toys to occupy himself with (see *Toys*, page 42). It will also be very useful when your children and their friends are rampaging around the house – and no, not as somewhere to shut them in! The puppy can be put in his kennel to stop him getting over-excited, and also to protect him from the possible unwanted attention of the children.

Many dog owners continue with the indoor kennel throughout the dog's life. If that is your intention, buy or build a kennel that is going to be big enough for your dog when he is fully grown. With my own breed – Bernese Mountain Dogs – the kennel I use whilst they are puppies is one and a half metres long, one metre wide and one metre high. Bearing in mind that they are only in the kennel when they are resting, this is quite big enough for them during the first six to nine months, and then I add on panels (1m x 1m), as necessary, to form an extension run. (Details of stockists for indoor kennels and extension panels are given on page 251.)

The indoor kennel should not be used to house the dog for the greater part of his day. It should simply be used as a secure area in which to leave him at bedtime, when you are out for an hour or so, or when you are busy indoors and cannot supervise him, until he is 'house-trained' in every sense of the word. With the extensions previously described, it is acceptable to leave the adult dog in the kennel for two to three hours at a time, but certainly not all day long.

Lastly, please do not use the indoor kennel as a place where you 'send' the dog to as punishment. The indoor kennel should be a place of comfort, calm and security – a place to which the dog has access twenty-four hours a day, so that, if he chooses, he can escape to his den for some rest and relaxation.

Indoor Kennels – Adult Dogs

If you are re-homing an adult dog, who may never have been in an indoor kennel, you will need to acclimatise the dog slowly to being confined – don't just shut him in there and expect him not to complain!

Have the kennel positioned in the place where it is to stay, set up with bedding and so on, the same as described for a puppy. Leave the kennel door open all the time. For the first few days, feed every meal to the dog inside the kennel, but *do not shut the door*. Place some interesting toys inside and slowly you will find that the dog goes into the kennel on his own accord, perhaps even lying down for a while. Don't be tempted to rush over and slam the door shut. Only when the dog has shown he is perfectly relaxed being inside, for up to twenty minutes, should you very casually push the door closed, but do not secure it. Keep the door closed for ten minutes, then just as casually, open it again. If, when you start to close the door, the dog immediately tries to rush out, don't react – let him come out if he wants to. Just wait until he is relaxed enough to venture in on his own once more, and start again.

So long as you don't rush the dog, within two to three weeks he will be quite happy to have the door secured behind him, and will remain in the kennel for an hour or so. Gradually build up the time until you can leave him in there whilst you go out for a couple of hours. As long as he has had a chance to relieve himself before going into the kennel, and has something safe to amuse himself with whilst in there, it will quickly become part of his routine.

Toys

All puppies and most adult dogs need toys to amuse themselves when left alone, and to interact with you during a 'playtime'. There is a multitude of choice in the pet shops, but you don't necessarily need to spend a fortune on things for your dog to play with. The cardboard roll innards of kitchen towel roll or toilet roll are super toys, and are something you usually throw away anyway. The dog can play with and chew it and you can use the cardboard roll to play 'fetch games' with the dog. Empty cardboard boxes are also great fun – after you have removed any staples or sticky paper, of course.

A couple of toys which you may like to buy are the 'educational' type. An example of these is a plastic cube which is hollow inside and has small holes on the outside. You can 'post' small treats inside the cube, and, as the puppy plays with it, every so often a treat appears. This can keep him amused for ages. There is also a rubber cone-shaped toy, advertised as being indestructible, with hollow insides. If you fill the hollow with soft dog food, it will keep the puppy concentrated for quite a while, as he licks the food out, much like a marrow bone. Please don't be tempted to give an adult dog or a puppy old shoes or slippers to play with. Apart from the danger of the dog swallowing them – possibly causing a severe internal blockage – it also teaches him to eat shoes, as he won't distinguish between old and new ones!

Collars and Leads
Puppies
You will initially need to buy just a soft collar and lead for your puppy. Don't be tempted to buy the best in the shop – it will only last for a few weeks, as the pup will soon outgrow it. It is basically needed to acclimatise the puppy to wearing a collar and being held gently on a lead. The collar should be put on the puppy as soon as you have brought him home. The lead should not be put on for a couple of weeks. Then it should be used as described in the section *Walking on the Lead*, page 140.

Adult Dogs
A nice leather or flat nylon collar, plus good-quality leather lead, are ideal for the adult dog. As soon as you take over ownership, you will need to fit a visible means of identification onto the dog's collar (see *Identification*,

page 199). If the dog you take on has already learned to pull hard when on a lead, an alternative to an ordinary collar is the head collar which is now readily available. The head collar is very similar to the halter worn by horses (not the bridle and bit type!) and although it can take the dog a little while to become accustomed to something around his head, it has proved very successful with some dogs who were previously strenuous pullers (see *Training*, page 107).

Collars and Leads for Formal Training
The first step is to select the right collar and lead. I would recommend you use a good-quality leather lead, at least three feet long, with a strong trigger-type clip for attaching the lead to the collar. Rope and nylon leads do not have the same flexible quality as leather and they can 'burn' your hands if pulled through quickly. As to collars, there are many types available:

TRAINING CHAINS
The training chain, or choke chain, is not favoured by most dog trainers and behaviourists. In extreme cases, incorrect fitting and usage can cause damage to the dog's neck. It certainly should NEVER be used on young puppies. Some experienced people do know how to use the chain correctly, but it is not necessary for a pet dog, and other softer collars are now available. However, because they *are* in use, the following information and diagrams are included on selecting a suitable one for your dog, fitting it and how to place it around the dog's neck.

The close-welded link variety is best, as it tends to run more freely through the links at each end. (The open-link variety can jam up.) The correct thickness is important – too thin and you will cut the dog's neck, too thick and it will be too heavy for the dog. When the chain is around the dog's neck, and adjusted so that it fits snugly (but NOT tightly), there should be about a hand's width of chain left, before it attaches to the lead.

Fig. 2. Incorrect (left) and correct (right) adjustment for a chain collar.

To put the chain on, position the dog next to you by your left leg, both of you facing the same direction. Form the collar into a circle by threading it through one metal ring. With the end that is going to be attached to the lead uppermost, slip the chain over the dog's head. Attach the lead to the free ring and, to check that you have it on correctly, use the lead to GENTLY tighten the collar, then relax the pressure. The collar should slacken instantly. If it doesn't, then the collar is on 'upside down'.

Finally, I repeat: the use of chain collars is unnecessary. Better and kinder collars are available.

ROPE AND NYLON SLIP COLLARS
These collars work in a similar way to a chain collar, but do not release around the neck very quickly, keeping the pressure on the dog's neck even after you have slackened the lead. This could have an adverse effect and actually hinder the training.

ORDINARY LEATHER COLLARS
Generally speaking, most puppies and adult dogs can be perfectly adequately trained wearing a normal leather collar. Because modern-day methods do not place the

emphasis on neck correction, there should not be a need for a special collar. If you can't manage on an ordinary collar, then a double action type, or the head collar, are the most acceptable.

Remember that, whatever type of collar your dog wears, it is a legal requirement that the collar must bear visible means of identification (even if your dog has been microchipped or tattooed). A small disc with your name and contact number and/or address should be attached to his collar.

DOUBLE ACTION TRAINING COLLAR
In my experience, if you want to use anything other than a leather collar, then this is the best type of training collar, suitable for the majority of dogs, including puppies. It is made of flat nylon, which is formed into a circle using a connection of a small length of chain, each end of the chain attaching to the nylon via a metal ring, with a third metal ring in the middle of the chain, for attaching the collar to the lead.

These collars are adjustable and come in various sizes, so they are suitable for the smallest of breeds to the largest. Make sure that you get the type with two

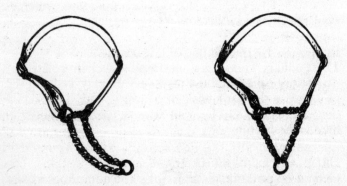

Fig. 3. A double action training collar showing (left) incorrect and right (correct) adjustment.

adjusters on it – you can buy them with only one adjuster, but these tend to slip and consequently need adjusting frequently.

When the collar is fitted around the dog's neck and the lead is attached, pull the lead gently so that pressure is applied to the collar and check that the two metal rings are not meeting. If they are, it means that there will be no 'give' in the collar and it will remain tight whether or not you are applying pressure via the lead. Use the adjusters so that when you do tighten the collar, at least half an inch of chain separates the two rings. That way, there is sufficient slack in the collar to relax it once pressure from the lead is stopped.

BODY HARNESSES
A harness may be recommended for a dog for medical reasons, e.g. if the dog has a neck problem. Unless it is for such a reason, I see no benefit in using one.

Feeding Your Dog or Puppy
You will need to have a supply of the food which the breeder of your puppy, or current keeper of the dog, is feeding. It is unwise to change the diet immediately you get the puppy or dog home. He has enough to cope with, settling into a new environment, without the risk of a tummy upset too. Have enough food for a few days, and then you can start to change the diet if you wish. More detailed information about how to feed your dog is given in Chapter 6, Feeding Your Dog, page 57.

Preparing the House and Garden
Before the dog or puppy comes home, have a close look at possible dangers around your home and outside in the garden. Make sure that any electrical wires are well tucked away, with nothing showing which a pup could either get caught up in, or pull down. Wastepaper bins should be put away from dog height, and shoes should be tidied away. Get into that routine NOW, so that it is automatic by the time the puppy arrives. Get the

children into the habit of keeping their bedroom doors closed too. If the children are used to leaving bags of crisps lying around, try and re-train them in advance of the dog's arrival.

Check the fences in the garden. Depending on the size of your dog, make sure that fences and walls will keep him in, not only from a height viewpoint, but also along the bottom of the fence: are there any small holes which the dog could squeeze through? Make sure that the dustbins are either shut away from access, or have properly fitting lids. Check carefully that any chemicals or fertilisers are locked safely away from inquisitive noses. If you have previously used such things as slug pellets in the garden, make sure that all traces are removed – they could kill your puppy. Protect any special shrubs or plants by fencing them off – puppies love to dig!

You can prepare a special area – a digging pit – where you can encourage the dog to dig, to protect those areas where you don't want him to. Choose the spot, about four foot by four foot, dig it over, clear stones, etc., maybe add some new soil to the area. Then bury a few suitable toys. When the puppy first goes into the garden, and after he has relieved himself, guide him to the digging pit, and start encouraging him to find the hidden toys, by digging with your hands and saying things like 'What's this?' and 'Where is it?'. It won't be long before the pup is scrabbling away with his paws, and when he finds the hidden toy, the reward will be enough to encourage him to dig again. If he is always encouraged to go to the digging pit, and discouraged by fences, etc. from the rest of the garden, you should be able to maintain the garden and keep the puppy happy at the same time!

Finally, don't forget to tell your neighbours about the prospective new arrival. If you warn them in advance that the dog may initially bark or howl at night-time, for example, it is less likely that you will have complaints from the neighbours later.

Choosing a Veterinary Surgeon

It is advisable to register with a veterinary surgeon before you bring your puppy home, just in case an emergency should arise where you will need a vet quickly. Take some time and ask other pet owners about their vet, so that you can get an idea which vet will suit you. Obviously, it is more convenient if you choose a practice fairly close to where you live, but it is important that you like the person who is going to be treating your dog, so perhaps you may decide on a practice a little further away, simply because you feel more able to communicate with that particular vet. Ideally, it would be nice if you could go and visit the practice and inspect the areas where your dog or puppy may be treated, such as the kennels and operating theatres. However, bear in mind that veterinary surgeries are busy places, regularly treating very sick animals, and it is therefore unlikely that the staff will be able to spare the time to show you around. Plus, the disturbance to patients, and the risk of bringing infection into the treatment areas, will probably make such a visit impractical. Don't assume that they have 'something to hide' simply because the practice will not allow you to look behind the scenes. Remember, it is possible that at some time during your dog's life, he could be the one who is disturbed, or put at risk, by potential clients 'wanting to view'!

5

Bringing the New Puppy or Dog Home

Travel Arrangements
It is best if you can arrange to collect the dog early in the day, so that you have as much time as possible with him before you have to settle him down for the first night away from either his mum and his siblings or, if you're getting a dog from a rescue centre, from the place which has meant security to him. Take a suitably-sized cardboard box, with a soft warm blanket, for a puppy to travel home in. Alternatively, you may want him to travel on someone's lap – if so, the person holding the puppy should not travel in the front seat. You should take towels, paper towels and plastic bags in case the puppy should have an upset stomach during the journey. Also, a container with fresh drinking water, plus a plastic bowl. Don't feed the puppy during the journey, or you will definitely be using the towels and plastic bags! The breeder should ensure that the puppy is fed well in advance of your arrival, so that the meal will have been digested before the journey. The same applies to adult dogs – the journey may upset them, and any undigested food in their stomach will not stay there long!

Paperwork from the Breeder
Before you leave the breeder, check that you have the pedigree for your puppy (if appropriate), diet sheet, and information on how often your puppy has been wormed. If you are buying a pedigree puppy, the

breeder should have registered the litter with the Kennel Club. You can expect to receive a transfer of ownership form, which you will need to send to the Kennel Club to re-register the puppy in your name, if not at the time you collect your puppy, then fairly soon afterwards, so make sure that it is all in hand before you leave for home.

Arriving Home

With a puppy, carry him in and take him straight through the house into the garden. He will undoubtedly be bursting to go to the toilet, and it will give you your first opportunity to start on the pup's house-training. Reward him when he does relieve himself and allow him to investigate his outside surroundings.

The adult dog will not need to be carried, but again he should be immediately taken to the garden, to establish from the beginning where he is allowed to relieve himself, and to prevent any accidents indoors on his first day.

The puppy will probably be quite tired after the journey, so, having already established where he will sleep, introduce him to his bed and allow him to rest. He may well simply flop onto any available floor space, but do make sure that he can rest without interruption from the children. Visitors to see the puppy should be put off until at least the next day, so that the puppy can settle.

The First Night

With puppies, it is quite natural for them to be a little restless on the first night in your home. Having already decided where the puppy is to sleep, and ensured that he has been fed and been to the toilet, you have to be a little hard-hearted when you hear the first little whine or bark. How you react now will set the pattern for the future. It is a normal human response to want to comfort the puppy, as you will feel sorry for him. What you MUST do, from now on, is think how the dog views *your* actions. If crying or barking provokes you into giving the puppy attention – however understandable it may be for you to want to reassure the puppy – he will view such attention as a reward for his action; that is, crying, whining or barking gets the humans to come to me. Yes, you'll feel rotten and perhaps guilty about ignoring the crying, but the puppy will settle eventually – sometimes within a few minutes, sometimes it may take longer. As each night goes by, you will find that the whining will get less and less, provided you are STRONG!

You can expect to be getting up earlier in the morning for a while! Usually, in the summer, as soon as it is light outside, or in the winter at the first sound the puppy hears, he will be awake and needing to spend a penny. As the puppy grows, you will find that he will sleep later (much like a baby), but in the early days, you should consider anything longer than five or six hours' sleep a positive bonus!

The First Few Days
With any new dog in the house, and particularly with a new puppy, you can expect the first few days to be quite exhausting, but nonetheless very satisfying. Everything which the puppy does will be a learning experience for you and him. Now is the time when you establish the ground rules, for both puppy and adult dog. Don't make the common mistake that so many new owners make, of letting the new dog do things now that you will not want, or accept, in the future. Letting a puppy 'get away' with behaviour because 'he's only a baby' will mean that your puppy, when grown into an adult dog, will still expect to be able to continue with that behaviour. If you are homing an adult dog, especially if the dog has had a bad time before you took him, your pity for him may tempt you to spoil him, perhaps by letting him sleep on the furniture, or sleeping on your bed. Dogs are opportunists and, if they are given privileges without really earning them, they will very quickly take over the role of boss, sometimes without you even

realising what is happening.

Don't immediately give the dog or puppy access to the entire house. Keep doors closed, or, if your house is open plan, gate off areas that you don't want the dog in. In the dog pack, only the top dog has access to all areas of the 'den'. The dog sees your house as the den, and by your restricting his access to it, he will quickly understand that he is not the top dog – the humans must be because they can go everywhere, whereas his access is limited (see also *Rank Structuring*, page 74).

Routine
It is important that you quickly establish a regular routine for the new dog or puppy. Sleeping, eating, playing and exercise (once the pup is able to go out) should all happen at around the same time every day. The children should be made to understand that the puppy is not always available to play with, and needs regular rest periods. Lack of a routine can hinder house-training, so eating, walking and sleeping should all happen in a regular pattern, allowing the puppy's head and body to get into a 'system'. The older dog will also need periods of quiet and a regular settled routine. (See also *Routines*, page 72.)

Visiting the Vet
Your new puppy will need to see your veterinary surgeon, for a general health check and for the first of his vital preventative vaccinations against distemper, hepatitis, leptospirosis, para influenza and parvo virus. The first vaccination will be given at eight to ten weeks of age, with the second at twelve weeks old. Your puppy should not mix with other dogs, or walk on the ground outside your house and garden until a week to ten days after the second vaccination. You will also need to obtain worming treatment for the puppy. The breeder of your puppy should already have started the worming procedure, and it needs to be continued until the puppy is six months old, and then every six months after that.

At that first visit, the vet will tell you at what age your puppy can be given his first treatment for the prevention of fleas. Even if your dog is an adult, it is as well to let your vet check him over, and the adult dog will still need both worm and flea prevention treatment.

Accompanying you and the new puppy or adult dog to the vet is a good way to start educating your children in caring for the new pet. However, please make sure that your children do not cause a nuisance to or disturb other clients and their animals. Many of the dogs, cats or other pets at the surgery will be either feeling unwell, or nervous, or both, and to have noisy children 'in their faces' simply adds to their discomfort, as well as possibly causing them to act out of character. The owners of these animals may also be feeling tense and worried, and so may not feel very tolerant of misbehaving children. Ensure that your children are aware of the situation, and that they will sit quietly without trying to stroke or talk to the other animals in the waiting room.

Microchip Identification
During your first trip to the vet, you can find out about microchipping your puppy. Microchipping is a permanent means of linking your dog to you. A small 'chip', about the size of a grain of rice, is injected between the dog's shoulder blades. It does not go right into the dog, but sits just under the skin. Each chip has an individual number which is recorded against your details and these details are held at a central base. The chip can be read by a small reader, much like a TV remote control. Many vets and most rescue centres have a reader, which they can then use to identify your dog if he is taken to them after being lost or straying.

If you have obtained your dog or puppy from a rescue centre, you may well find that the dog has already been microchipped, as many of them now provide that service before the dog goes to his new home.

As previously mentioned, even if you have your dog microchipped, it is still a legal requirement that he has a visible means of identification. A small disc, with *your* name and a contact number and/or address etched onto it, should be attached to his collar.

Visitors

Family and friends will obviously want to come and see the new puppy, but encourage them to come at a time when the puppy will be having a playtime, rather than disturbing a much needed rest period. It is also important that visitors know how to greet the new puppy. It is human nature to want to cuddle the puppy as soon as they arrive at the front door, but if you want to avoid problems in the future, it is best to establish from the start where the puppy is to be greeted, and the front door is not the best place! Most importantly, it could be extremely dangerous, as the puppy could get out. Holding the puppy back, or picking him up is not the answer either. Whilst you want the puppy to be sociable, if visitors are allowed to pet and give attention to the puppy as soon as they walk in the door, you have the potential for the dog becoming incredibly spoiled, getting everything he asks for and being a pain to live with! You do not want your puppy to think that he is the most important member of the household, which he soon will if every new person who visits the house gives him attention immediately, almost before stepping over the threshold.

Establish from the beginning that when visitors arrive, the puppy should remain in the kitchen. The visitors can then be invited into the house safely, without risk to the puppy from an open front door. Then bring the visitors into the kitchen, but ask them not immediately to fall onto their knees to say hello to the pup. If the puppy is leaping around, trying to get attention, ask the visitors to ignore him. Settle the visitors, perhaps at the kitchen table, and, once the puppy has stopped trying to get their attention, invite them to say hello to the puppy. It is difficult, I know, for people to ignore a cuddly bundle of puppy, but it will be worth it in the long run. If you start off this way, you will avoid a situation which many people will recognise – that of having a dog 'in your face' as soon as you step into the house. The pup will quickly learn two things – he is not greeted at the front door, so will be more likely to take himself into the kitchen where he knows he will be petted, and also that the way to get attention is not to demand it.

6

Feeding Your Dog

Knowing what to feed your dog can prove to be very confusing. Every dog expert has his own particular favourite canine diet and there is now such a vast selection of dog food available that it can be quite bewildering for the first-time dog owner to decide what to feed. Fresh, tinned, dried, vacuum-packed – the list is endless. Obviously, puppies have different food requirements from adult dogs, so make sure that you feed the proper puppy diet from the food range you choose.

The majority of pet shops and many vets will probably advise feeding your new puppy or adult dog on a complete dried food, which is considered nutritionally balanced. Some will suggest feeding tinned food, or vacuum-packed meat-based products. These types of food are many and varied and are advertised as being suitable. Indeed, most of the advertising will suggest that it is the only way to feed your dog if you want him or her to have a long and healthy life. To discuss each and every variety of manufactured dog food available today would take a book on its own! However, before you make your choice, I would like to give you another choice – a **NATURAL** diet, structured on what your dog would eat if living in the wild, and the diet that your dog's most recent and still surviving ancestor, the wolf, lives on.

It is a diet based mainly on **raw meaty bones!** It is the diet that most people fed to their dogs up until the last thirty or forty years, when the commercial pet food market really erupted. It is the diet that your dog is 'designed' to eat: dogs have the teeth to shred, rip and tear flesh and crunch bones, and stomachs designed to digest both raw bones and raw meat. This is what I feed my dogs on, and more and more people are coming back to this well tried and tested way of feeding dogs. Dogs are essentially *carnivores*, which means that their main diet largely consists of meat and bone. They *may* occasionally eat the stomach contents of their prey, i.e. partly digested vegetable matter, but it is not a vital part of their diet and they do not need it.

Most vets will recommend one of the commercial diets, as the instructions are on the can or packet. They do not have the time, during a normal consultation, to explain about the benefits of natural feeding, or to give advice as to quantities, etc. Some vets sell dried dog food, so therefore will obviously recommend it. Some pet food manufacturers sponsor vet colleges, so therefore the alternative ways of feeding are not given priority, or worse still, are not discussed, so the veterinary students don't learn about them. Indeed, many dog owners are told that raw, uncooked bones are bad for their dogs! The convenience of opening a tin, or scooping out a couple of mugfuls of dried pellets is simple, requiring little or no thought, which suits the busy lives which many owners lead.

The fact that there is now a massive, multi-billion pound industry, which effectively tells dog owners that they (the owners) couldn't possibly work out how and what to feed their dogs on their own, has led to increasing numbers of owners accepting that the pet food manufacturers must know best, and being drawn into buying commercially prepared foods and artificial bones. All tinned and processed foods have been cooked, and the resulting changes in the structure of the food means that the dog's digestive system has to work much harder, as it is designed to digest **raw** ingredients. Then there is the major effect that cooked processed foods have on the dog's teeth. The majority of dogs fed on an artificial diet will need to have their dirty teeth and infected gums attended to by a vet several times during their lives. The processed food gets stuck in the teeth, causing infection. Just take a look at your own teeth after you've eaten a biscuit – that is what your dog's teeth look like after eating dried, pelleted food! Even using artificially produced teeth-cleaning products will leave a deposit on the dog's teeth. Bacteria enter the body through the diseased and infected teeth and gums, and can set up chronic infections which later may result in liver, heart or kidney problems. Cleaning your dog's teeth with a toothbrush will not remove all the gunge – and, honestly, how many people are going to clean their dogs' teeth properly twice a day? By eating raw bones, the dogs floss their own teeth in the ripping and shredding action. The only teeth that need to be artificially cleaned are the canine teeth, which are the teeth designed for killing the prey, and are not involved in the ripping and grinding motion. I clean my dogs' canine teeth once or twice a week with an electric toothbrush, and, if you start from puppyhood, they will quickly get used to it.

If you have an adult dog and want to change to feeding naturally, take a look at the state of his teeth first. If the dog's teeth are already in poor condition, he will be unable to crush the bones properly and his gums may also hurt too, so have his teeth cleaned properly, by your veterinary surgeon. That way, he will be starting with a 'clean slate'.

Diet affects temperament too. Some dogs fed on commercially produced food are continually hyped up by the additives in the food, or by the turmoil in their guts, trying to digest vitamins, etc. which have been chemically changed during the cooking process. During the course of my dog training life, I have often been asked to visit dogs with, as the owners report, behavioural problems, only to find that a suggested diet change usually sorts out most of the perceived problems. Natural feeding of raw meaty bones is especially beneficial for dogs with skin problems too.

Another positive benefit of natural feeding is what comes out of the other end of the dog, as waste matter. Because the dog can easily digest the natural diet, there is far less wastage, and what is eliminated is much less offensive and much easier to pick up. The faeces of a bone-fed dog are solid, unlike the revolting concoction that comes from a dog fed on some of the most high profile branded foods.

Initially, it takes more thought and forward planning to feed your dog on a natural diet, but you will quickly get into the routine, and knowing that you are feeding the best possible food for your dog is enough of a reward.

Meat and Bones

Approximately 60 to 70 per cent of the daily food ration should comprise raw meaty bones, such as chicken wings and chicken carcasses (frames). With a little research you should be able to find a butcher who is prepared to supply you with the carcasses, and chicken wings can be purchased either there, or at the super-market. To begin with, a puppy of seven weeks will not be able to break through the whole bone of the chicken wing or carcass, so break it down first, with a meat tenderiser, or mince it. The puppy will quickly increase his jaw strength and, even before the adult teeth come through at about fifteen weeks, he will be able to break through the bone.

When changing an adult dog over to raw feeding, you can supplement with raw meat – chicken, beef, rabbit, lamb – but don't get stuck into the habit of just feeding raw meat. It is raw meat ON THE BONE that is so important to your carnivore's teeth, gums and overall health. You can also feed raw fish too.

Additionally, start him off with a **jointed** bone daily. He will not be able to break through the bone but the gnawing will help strengthen his jaws, keep the baby teeth clean and the gums healthy. He will also get huge enjoyment from it! The look on a puppy's face when he is gnawing on a bone is just wonderful! When he starts to lose his baby teeth and the adult teeth start to come through, regular bone gnawing and chewing will help the teething process no end. Once he has his full set of adult teeth, plus stronger jaws, he will be able to eat the bone completely – beef and lamb bones are best. Marrow bones are useful only as a recreational bone – the bone is too hard for even an adult dog to do much with.

When you begin feeding raw bones, it is best to supervise your dog, to ensure that he eats them safely; dogs who have not previously had access to bones may sometimes get so excited at having real food that they may try to swallow large pieces whole. If necessary, hold the bone to begin with, so that the dog gets the hang of chewing on it, rather than trying to eat it in one go! Until your puppy has the jaw strength to break through the bone, let him gnaw on it for an hour or so, them pick it up, rinse it under the cold tap, and store it in a plastic bag in the fridge. It will last for two to three days this way. Bones can also be fed frozen – indeed, in the summer my dogs prefer them this way, with no detriment to their health!

Raw meat on the bone, whole carcasses and meaty bones are the main and most important part of this diet. The foods listed below are useful additions.

Vegetables

If you wish, you can feed your dog small amounts of crushed raw vegetables, but it is not essential and some dogs do not like vegetables at all. If you do feed vegetables, you must crush them because vegetables are surrounded by a cellulose wall, and dogs cannot digest cellulose. Using a liquidizer or food processor, pulp the vegetables to a paste, thereby breaking down the cellulose. If you start your puppy off with a small amount, he will probably accept it, but please don't feel that your dog must have veggies; and if he doesn't want it, don't give it to him!

Start with a teaspoon of pulped raw vegetable added to one daily meal. Use any vegetable available **EXCEPT ONION** (which is toxic to dogs) and **NOT CORN ON**

THE COB (the cob cannot be digested and may get stuck in the gut), and be sparing with the broad-leaved vegetables, such as cabbage, etc. Garlic and parsley added to the mix are beneficial.

Fruit

Give fruit (pulped) in a similar way, making sure that there aren't any pips or stones in the pulp. You can also use fruit as a treat or titbit. **DO NOT GIVE GRAPES OR RAISINS TO YOUR DOG. IN SUFFICIENT QUANTITIES, THEY CAN CAUSE KIDNEY FAILURE. The toxic dose of grapes for a dog weighing 50 lb is just 10 oz; for raisins it is less, because they are just concentrated grapes.**

Other Foods

You can give your puppy sensible table scraps too, as well as things such as yoghurt, cottage cheese, scrambled or raw eggs, including the shell (not too many). On a natural, biologically appropriate diet, your puppy does not need cereals or dog biscuits. Don't feed any food containing refined sugar either. All these types of food are extras; if you don't want to feed your dog anything other than raw meaty bones, he or she will be perfectly satisfied and glowing with health.

How Much Food to Feed

It is difficult to tell you how much to feed your individual puppy or adult dog. As a rough guide, he should be having about 20 per cent of his total target body weight in food **over one week**. For example:

Weight of Dog	Amount of Food **per week**
9kg (approx. 19 lb)	1.8kg (approx. 3.5 lb)
18kg (approx. 38 lb)	3.6kg (approx. 7.6 lb)
50kg (approx. 110 lb)	10kg (approx. 22 lb)

To begin with you must use your common sense, and either increase or decrease the amount depending on how the puppy is growing and what he or she weighs. Weigh him every week so you can keep a check on his progress. Puppies grow at an amazing rate, so they need proportionately more food as they get older. Once your dog is fully grown, you will need to level out the amounts, and sometimes actually reduce them. As a guide to how much your particular puppy may need, the following is the diet I gave my most recent Bernese Mountain Dog puppy – but please bear in mind that, as an adult dog, a Bernese will weigh anything up to 110 lb (50 kilos), so if you have a small dog, reduce the amounts accordingly!

Diet for Bernese Puppy at 10 weeks
BREAKFAST
3 scrambled eggs with one slice brown of bread **OR** 2/3 sardines in oil mashed up with a tablespoonful of cottage cheese **OR** small tin of tuna fish in oil with either bread or cottage cheese.

LUNCH
2 mashed-up chicken wings; dessertspoonful of pulped mixed vegetable; teaspoonful of natural low-fat yoghurt afterwards; small raw jointed bone to chew on – either lamb or beef.

I usually left him with the bone (supervised) for an hour. At ten weeks old the jaws and teeth are not really strong enough to eat the actual bone, but he had great pleasure in gnawing on it and it was excellent exercise for the jaw, neck and chest area, plus, of course, it was brilliant for his teeth, especially when the adult teeth were breaking through.

LATE AFTERNOON
Same as breakfast.

MID-EVENING
3 mashed-up chicken wings.

Once a day he had a teaspoonful of honey – licked directly from the spoon! I also started to introduce small amounts of table scraps: teaspoonful of mashed potato, leftover meat from roast dinner, sausage, toast, etc. He also started having small amounts of fruit and cheese as titbits for training.

Diet for Bernese Puppy at 14 weeks
I now reduced him to three meals a day, as follows:

BREAKFAST
2 chicken wings **OR** either tuna or sardines with cottage cheese, tablespoonful of pulped vegetable.

LUNCH
3 chicken wings (whole, fed on the ground as he was crunching them properly); tablespoonful of yoghurt afterwards; a couple of times a week he had a raw egg, with shell.

MID-AFTERNOON
Two or three times a week he had a raw bone mid-afternoon (he could now manage to eat the ends off!).

ABOUT 7.00 PM
3 chicken wings **OR** 1 chicken frame (carcass) (fed on the ground); plus table scraps as appropriate and when available; plus fruit and cheese for titbits; plus dessert-spoonful of honey two or three times a week.

Diet for Adult Bernese
BREAKFAST
2 chicken frames; tablespoonful of yoghurt afterwards.

EARLY EVENING
3 or 4 chicken frames **OR** whole oxtail **OR** whole rabbit **OR** half a chicken **OR** whole lamb neck with rib cage

OR a lump of lamb on the bone.

I still give fruit and cheese as titbits, and he still has a tablespoonful of honey once or twice a week.

I tend to feed my dogs their main bone meal once the sun has gone down; this is simply because in the summer the flies tend not to be so prolific at that time of day and, as the food is fed directly on the ground, it reduces the risk of infection, etc.

The list can vary, depending on what is available. Weight and amounts fed on a daily basis can also vary. For example, a lump of lamb on the bone weighs about 2½ lb (just over 1kg), whereas the carcasses weigh between 10–12 oz (310–375g) each. However, it balances out over a week or so. In the wild, dogs would not eat exactly the same amount every day, and there would be days when they would not get a kill, so they would go hungry. Some dog owners who subscribe to the natural diet actually fast their dogs for one day a week, to try to replicate what would happen in the wild.

Allowing for obvious differences in amounts fed for a smaller dog, don't feel that you must follow the diet slavishly – everyone has his own preferences – and once you have done all the research, you may want to adjust it as you see fit. Most importantly though, remember that the bone part of the diet is just as important as the meat part, and the best way to feed the two is as one 'lump' of meat on the bone. Some people think of bone as waste – it isn't. **It is food!**

Sourcing the Food
As previously mentioned, much of the food can be obtained from the supermarket. However, I would strongly recommend that you find a butcher to supply you. In that way, you can find out exactly where the meat, etc. is coming from – often it will be a local supplier. Ideally, an organic source is best, but costs may rule this out.

Precautions

As you will be handling raw meat, and your dog will be eating it, there are a few sensible hygiene and safety precautions you should take:

- Worm your dog every two months, after the initial puppy worming.
- Scald all bowls and utensils with **boiling** water, after normal washing.
- Clean the ground outside after bone eating, and remove shards of bone.
- Store all raw foods separately from other foods.
- Store the food in plastic containers whilst it is defrosting.
- Supervise all bone meals until the puppy is eating them properly.
- Wash your hands **before** and **after** preparing raw meals.
- The canine teeth are not used for grinding bone, and therefore do not get cleaned: clean them with a cloth or soft brush at least weekly.
- Large dogs sometimes try to eat chicken wings whole, in one lump. You can stop this by holding the food as they eat, but perhaps it is easier and better to feed them the larger chicken frames.

Pros of Natural Feeding

The following list is just a few of the enormous benefits that result from feeding a natural diet:

1. A much healthier dog, so fewer trips to the vet.
2. A much happier dog.
3. A dog with good, strong, clean teeth, with no gum disease.
4. A dog with pleasant smelling breath.
5. A dog whose behaviour isn't being 'hyped up' by artificial foods.
6. A dog whose 'waste product' is much less offensive and much easier to pick up!

Cons of Natural Feeding

It would be irresponsible if I did not point out the few possible downsides of natural feeding:

1. Possible risk of impaction – very rare but could happen.

2. Arguing the case for natural feeding with your vet. Try and convert him or her; lend him or her the books!

3. When you first start feeding naturally, it takes a little more thought and time than feeding processed food – but it gets easier very quickly!

4. You may occasionally notice a very slight smear of blood in the faeces. This is usually caused by a small piece of undigested bone 'scratching' as it is eliminated.

5. If you are changing over from feeding a processed, artificial diet, it is not unusual for your dog to have an upset stomach for a couple of days. This is because the stomach of the dog has had to unlearn how to make the best of a bad job, coping with cooked and processed food. Once you start feeding the raw diet, the stomach will quickly start working at full efficiency again.

Read and research as much as possible about raw feeding; don't just take my word for it! Go onto the Internet and search. Start with Tom Lonsdale's website (see Appendix, page 252). Read his book; it will change the way you think about feeding your dog for ever – it certainly did for me! There are other websites where you can get help and information; you will find that people who have changed over to natural feeding love to share their experiences with others!

Buy the books, talk to other dog owners who feed naturally. Be prepared to be told that you're wrong! Some vets (often the younger ones) have only ever known about processed feeding, because the natural way was either not encouraged or not talked about at all when they were studying. Some butchers will tell you NOT to feed bones to your dog and especially not chicken. Some dog owners will tell you that you're being cruel and that you will harm your dog. **Become an expert at feeding your dog naturally and convert them!**

How to Serve the Food

The answer to this one may seem glaringly obvious, but if you are feeding all or part of your dog's food in a bowl, only small or medium-size dogs should eat with their bowl directly on the floor. Dogs of a Labrador's size and upwards should ideally be fed with their bowl placed in a stand at shoulder height to the dog. This can aid the journey of the food to the dog's stomach, and can help to avoid gastric dilation (see page 196) Unlike humans, who need to chew food to prompt the digestive juices to start flowing, the dog's digestive juices do not start to work until the food reaches the stomach. Dogs therefore gulp their food down and, as a consequence, take in large amounts of air as they eat. With the larger dog, if he is fed with his bowl on the floor, the food has to travel upwards first, before passing down into the dog's stomach, so even more air is taken in to assist the food on its journey. For the same reasons, it is always best to feed your adult dog twice a day, rather than give

Fig. 4. Larger dogs should be fed at shoulder height.

him one huge meal. Puppies, of course, will be fed from between four and six meals a day to begin with.

If you are feeding a natural diet, then most of the dog's food will be fed outside on the ground, and the dog will lie down to eat it; save the feeding stand for the raw meat, vegetables, etc.

Titbits

Dogs cannot digest refined sugar, so please do not give them biscuits and snack food sold for human consumption. Titbits are really best reserved as a backup for training when you should either use the proprietary branded type or, better still, small pieces of apple or cheese. NEVER give your dog chocolate that is designed for human consumption. Dark chocolate is especially bad for dogs – it contains a substance called theobromine, which is a bitter, white crystalline alkaloid, related to caffeine and found in cocoa. It is a heart stimulant and could cause your dog serious problems. Theobromine is also found in cocoa shell mulch, the type of mulch that is used for many pot plants, so be aware that any potted plants that you buy may also present a real danger to your dog.

Possessiveness with Food

You will rapidly discover that food is your dog's number one priority! That said, an early and vital part of your establishing yourself as the leader is by showing him that he can only have his food at your discretion and command. Some dogs are never possessive with food, but you may find that if your dog came from a large litter, the way he obtained his share was by threatening his brothers and sisters. If such action achieved the desired result, i.e. getting more food, he may well try that with you. If you don't sort this out very early on, this possessiveness will transfer to other things, such as bones, toys, furniture and so on, perhaps even to members of the family.

To stop him being aggressive with his food, don't give

him possession of it! In other words, feed him by hand for at least a couple of weeks. Prepare his food in the bowl as usual, but don't put the bowl on the floor for him. Simply feed him a handful at a time. The presence of the bowl of food on the floor almost instinctively makes him want to guard it, so if he is not put in the position of needing to guard, he will not bite! Feeding him by hand also helps if your dog is dominant in other areas. It makes him completely reliant on you for the most important thing in his life, i.e. food, and will therefore reinforce your position as pack leader, since he is only getting the food from you, not from a bowl. You can also use the period of hand feeding to reinforce your control further, by making him perform some minor order from you for some of the food. Get him to sit first before one handful, or to lie down for the next, and so on. Obviously, don't make him run about for the food – that could lead to digestive upsets, or worse. Sedentary acts, however, will not do him any harm.

You will find that, after a couple of weeks of this regime, his general demeanour over possessions will alter. You can then try giving him his food in a bowl again, and, provided there is positively no sign of aggression, continue to feed normally.

For dogs that are food possessive, do not give them bones or toys until you have overcome the problem, as they will attempt to guard these in the same way. Once the food possession has been sorted out, you can try introducing a toy, but make sure the dog understands that it is *your* toy, which he is allowed to play with only with you, and when *you* decide that the game is to end, *you* always end up with the toy. Again, once he is OK with toys, you can then introduce a bone. (See also *Mouthing and Biting – Puppies*, page 97.)

7

The First Few Weeks

Boundaries
One of the earliest lessons your dog has to learn when
he enters your home is where his boundaries are. By this,
I mean what you are going to allow him to get away
with. If you don't want him on the furniture, for example, then don't let him start. If he has already requisi-
tioned a chair and you would rather he hadn't, simply
tip the chair over, without saying anything, and evict
him. If he gets back up, repeat the procedure until he
gives in. DON'T reward him when he gets off – he
shouldn't have been up there in the first place.

Don't make the mistake of treating him as you would
a naughty child. There is an important difference
between the two – a child has the ability to reason, a dog
hasn't. You can explain to a naughty child why he is
receiving punishment and he will understand. Dogs do
not understand language and do not understand physical punishment, as in pack life to hurt another member
of the pack is counter-productive – all members needing
to be fit and strong so that the whole pack continues to
thrive.

Over the next few weeks, it is vital that you show the
dog, in a logical way, where he fits within the family
group. Today, more and more owners are consulting
dog behaviourists because the dog is exhibiting behaviour which they don't like, even whilst the dog is still
just a few months old. The most common reason why
unacceptable behaviour develops is that the dog is
acting like a dog, and the owner tries to apply human

71

logic to the problem, rather than understanding how the dog interprets *our* behaviour.

Routines

Because any upset in routine can cause possible problems with house-training, it is important that early on you establish a regular routine for your dog. All the important things in his life should happen in a regular pattern, such as eating, walking and sleeping, allowing his head and his body to get into a 'system'. Imagine the effect on his stomach if you fed him at 8 am on one day and at 2 pm the next. His stomach would soon get very upset, as would his sleeping and toilet routine.

The same thing happens if there is no regularity in his life and no consistency over what he is and is not allowed to do. He can only adapt into the human way of life if he has a regular timetable, i.e. feeding, sleeping, exercise, playing, being left, etc. Even though it is not ideal for you to leave your dog all day whilst you go to work, he can adjust to long periods of being alone – although, of course, you will have to make sure that the time he does spend with you is as full and interesting as possible.

As well as the routine of the household, you should get him into a regular routine of being brushed and 'looked at'. (See also Chapter 12, page 181.) Examining your dog may sound strange, but if you get him used to his ears being checked, his teeth, eyes, feet, etc., all being held and examined, it will make your job, and that of the vet, much easier when the dog is unwell and in need of attention. It is very difficult, for example, to bandage up a cut paw when the dog won't let you near his feet!

Get used to the look and feel of him when he is healthy, so that you will quickly be able to spot when something is wrong. For those of you who have a female dog, make sure you know what her intimate parts look like, so that you will be able to see the difference when she starts her season. If you don't know how to tell when she is in season, by the time you do notice, it may be too late – she may already be pregnant!

Inconsistent Behaviour
It is important that you are consistent with what you are
going to allow your dog to do. As an example, on a nice,
dry, sunny day, the dog comes in from the garden and is
allowed straight through into the rest of the house. On a
wet day, when the dog will have wet and muddy feet, in
he comes, attempts to continue his usual pattern of
going into the rest of the house, and, because we don't
want muddy paw marks on the carpet, we shout and
scream, perhaps slamming the door in his face. To us,
this is very logical, but to the dog, who doesn't have any
understanding of the difference between dirty carpet
and clean carpet, he sees our behaviour as unpredictable
– one day he is allowed in the entire house, the next he is
told off for repeating the same routine.

We confuse dogs with our inconsistencies – at home
we play with them on the floor, we make 'baby' sounds
at them in a soft and loving voice. Outside in the park,
where people may be watching and we don't want to be
thought of as soft, we don't play with them, don't talk
lovingly to them – indeed we may be rather gruff-voiced.
We try to be leader of the pack, but when our dog tries
to initiate a 'pack' hunt, and rolls in the droppings of
the animal to be hunted, like fox or deer, we get very
cross, shouting and rushing at him to stop doing it.

At home, we may encourage him to climb on our lap,
or jump up at us for a welcome or a cuddle. When
visitors call and the dog attempts to repeat the same,
previously encouraged behaviour with the visitor, we are
embarrassed, and tell him to get off. We may accidentally drop some human food onto the floor and call the
dog to come and clean it up – we then get cross when
the dog attempts to eat the same smelling food from the
kitchen worktop!

All these examples – and there are many more –
completely confuse the dog. We must therefore look at
how our actions are interpreted by the dog, and NOT

73

attribute the dog with human values. If we don't, mistrust and misunderstanding are built up, seriously affecting our ability to train our dogs.

Lifestyles and Rank Structuring
The way dogs are kept today is very different from when I was a child. Then, the dog was either kept outside in a kennel, or at least confined to the kitchen. Very occasionally the dog was allowed into the living accommodation, and he was *never* allowed upstairs. Because homes were not centrally heated, doors were kept closed to retain heat, and therefore the dog was not given access to the rest of the house – only by special invitation. Whilst that is certainly not the way I like to keep my dogs, what it did demonstrate very clearly to the dog was his position within the household. The humans had access to all areas, whereas he was only allowed in certain areas – his understanding of that situation was that he was lower in rank than the humans. As a result, the dog, knowing his position, did not attempt to 'take rank', nor try and dominate with shows of aggression or attention-seeking behaviour.

With more people going out to work full-time, many dogs are left alone for up to eight hours a day. Dogs are naturally gregarious – they need company – and left alone for hours on end they become bored, stressed and destructive. When the owners come home in the evening, the dog is so thrilled with having company that he gets over-excited, perhaps hyperactive, and the owners just can't cope with the attention which the dog is naturally demanding. Walking the dog becomes a chore which has to be fitted into an already hectic life, rather than an enjoyable time for dog and owner to interact.

Often, the first thing the owner does when returning home from work is to feed the dog – perhaps because of guilt at having left the dog alone. It may be that he or she wants to get the feeding 'out of the way', so as to concentrate on preparing the family meal. No matter what the reason, the dog views his feeding as being more important than the human's, because he is fed first. His pack understanding tells him that the most important member of the pack eats first.

Years ago, only a few households had access to a car, so the dog was walked everywhere, satisfying two very important needs: *socialising*, by meeting people and encountering different situations (perhaps on the daily walk to school with the children), and *exercise*, stimulating and enjoyable time spent bonding with the family. Nowadays, the dog tends to travel to the park by car and the children travel to school by car, so the dog's world is reduced considerably, limiting both mental and physical exercise.

There are procedures which you can implement to ensure that your puppy or adult dog understands where he fits within your family group. Not all of the suggestions have to be carried on forever, but simply put in place until your dog is at a level which is acceptable to you and the family.

1. Confine the dog to one room in the house for a few minutes every day. This is not meant as a punishment, so don't be gruff or unkind when you shut him away. This simply shows the dog that he cannot always be with you or follow you around. Ignore barking and whining and scratching at the door, and don't let him out whilst he is making a noise.

2. Don't allow him to occupy key areas in the house – doorways and the top of the stairs are all areas that should be controlled by the leader of the pack and, if your dog sees himself as higher ranked, he will feel it is his place to control these areas. Height especially is associated with rank. Your bed, or on the furniture, and as already mentioned, the top of the stairs, are all important areas to the dog to take or maintain his position of rank. Make these areas inaccessible to the dog – put a stair-gate across the bottom of the stairs, keep bedroom doors closed and deny access to furniture. Tip up chairs in the

Fig. 5. Don't allow your dog to occupy key areas in the house.

lounge, or cover the seats with kitchen foil (dogs do not like the sound or feel of foil under their feet). Block access to the settee.

3. For a few minutes every day, for a couple of weeks, sit in the dog's bed or den! Make sure the dog can see you. Yes, you'll feel very silly, but it is important for you to show the dog that you can occupy any area, and that he does not have 'ownership' or right over any place or thing – the bed is yours, and you allow him to use it!

4. Eat before the dog does. The dog understands that higher ranked individuals eat first. If your meal times do not coincide with the dog's, then at least have a snack or eat a biscuit before you put the dog's food down for him to eat.

5. Always make the dog move out of your way, never step over or walk around him. Again, the dog's understanding is that lower ranked individuals have to make way for those with higher rank.

6. Don't succumb to demands for attention. Dogs learn to do this in many ways – nudging your arm for a stroke, pawing at you, jumping up, continually

bringing toys to you. Any contact should always be instigated by you, and then earned by getting the dog to do something for you first – a simple **sit** is enough – before you give him a fuss.

7. Toys. The dog should have access to toys when he is left alone, but when you are in the house toys should only be made available when you are going to play with the dog. You want the dog to understand that they are *your* toys (as a lower ranked individual he has access to nothing, unless you give him permission). Select a toy, have a game and then take back possession of the toy. Some dogs, even very young puppies, can display aggressive signs with tug-of-war games – try to avoid this type of toy, and do not let the children play tuggy games with the dog.

8. Always insist that you go through a doorway first, and don't allow the dog to barge past you.

9. Every day, have a light training session with the dog for a few minutes – sit, down and stand, and eventually stay. This will not only help the dog to learn these basic exercises, but it again gives you the opportunity of some quality bonding time with him.

As the dog accepts his position within the family, you may wish to introduce more privileges and allow the dog more access to the family areas. Provided the dog does not take advantage and view these privileges as a sign of your weakness, there is no harm in bringing the dog to a level at which *you* are happy. Some people do not mind their dogs being on the furniture, for example, but it is so important that your dog understands that you are giving him that access, as opposed to him taking it.

House-Training
Puppies
One of the first routines to be established with any new puppy, and perhaps with some adult dogs, is where and when it is appropriate to relieve himself. Please accept

77

that there will be some accidents indoors, and please DO NOT punish the puppy or even the adult dog for these accidents.

Going to the toilet is a normal bodily function and, as far as a dog is concerned, especially a puppy, when they need to go, they go where they happen to be! The fact that the 'delivery' of either urine or faeces on the carpet is obnoxious to us is a concept that dogs do not understand. The 'old wives' tale' of rubbing the dog's nose in the mess (ugh!) or throwing the puppy outside, so they will learn that it is wrong, is completely misguided. The fact that puppies treated in such a manner do eventually become house-trained is more luck than anything else – they would have become house-trained anyway. What such treatment *does* do is build up mistrust between human and dog as, in the dog's mind, such behaviour is illogical and makes humans even more difficult to understand.

Bearing in mind that the puppy will need to go to the toilet frequently, it is up to you to ensure that when that need arises, the puppy is in an appropriate place to perform the required action. As such, take the puppy into the garden as soon as he wakes from sleeping, as soon as he has eaten, after a playtime, and every hour apart from that! The need to visit the garden will reduce as the number of mealtimes is reduced – remember that at seven weeks old your puppy may be having up to six meals per day, which will gradually be reduced to two by the time he is about six months old.

Note that I said *take* the puppy into the garden – if you simply put him outside unsupervised, he may go to the toilet, or he may simply play and sniff, quickly forgetting what he is out there to do. This could well result in him coming indoors and peeing on the carpet! If you are not outside with him to reward him, he will not learn that going to the toilet outside pleases you, whereas when he performs the same action indoors, it gets ignored. If you use small food treats for rewarding him outside as soon as he 'empties', at the same time using a simple sound, like 'Be quick' or 'Hurry up', you will quickly be able to get him to go to the toilet on command, as he will associate that sound with his action, plus the reward at the end of said action.

To begin with, you may find that you have to stay outside with the puppy for quite a while before he performs the required action. Don't be tempted into a game with the pup, or he will never do what is required. Without losing sight of him, try and ignore him, removing any toys he may bring to you in an attempt to get you to play. Don't get cross or impatient – it may be cold, raining and thundering, but he still needs to go to the toilet.

If you choose to train the puppy to use newspaper indoors to begin with, you will eventually successfully house-train him, but it will take a little longer, as you will have to 'de-train' him from the paper first. Unless your puppy is unrestricted at night-time, in which case he will have access to the floor, I would suggest that you don't use newspaper indoors.

When the puppy is old enough to go out on exercise, you can continue with the sound he will have learned in the garden, and the puppy will quickly understand where it is appropriate to go to the toilet, rather than embarrass you by going on the pavement – and remember, wherever he does relieve himself outside, don't forget to clean up after him!

Adult Dogs

Sometimes adult dogs will forget their house-training – either through trauma or perhaps because, if they were in a rescue centre, they have spent some time in a kennel environment when they could relieve themselves where they liked. Much of the previous advice on house-training puppies works just as well with the adult dog. It is so important to remember that any 'accidents' are not deliberate, and that the dog is not wrong, just a bit confused because of his new surroundings. Punishment for mistakes on the carpet will simply lead to the dog becoming bewildered at your attitude and perhaps more secretive about where indoors he does his toilet.

Occasionally, a newly re-homed adult male dog will attempt to 'territory mark' his new home, by cocking his leg on the corners of furniture, doors and so on, thereby leaving his scent for other dogs to know he is there, and also to reassure himself that his new home smells of him. Again, punishment will not solve the problem. Obviously, ensure that you clean the areas thoroughly and, where possible, move the 'inviting' pieces of furniture to less strategic places. The quickest way to stop this territory marking is to settle the dog into a proper routine immediately, letting the dog know where his boundaries are, and ensuring that at the same time he receives plenty of loving reassurance when he goes to the toilet in the appropriate place.

Getting Clean Throughout the Night
Getting the dog clean through the day is relatively easy, but the long period during the night can be a problem.

This could be for a variety of reasons. Sometimes, the young dog has simply not yet learnt to control himself and here you can try putting newspapers on the floor just for night-time use. It could be that he is 'asking' to go out and has been unable to attract your attention. If this is the case, it may be worth setting your alarm clock a couple of times during the night, just for a week or two, so that you can let him out. Admittedly this will mean a broken night's sleep for you but, if the end justifies the means, so be it. Perhaps he has learned that if he stands by the back door, he is let into the garden, but of course at night-time nobody can see him as everyone's in bed. (See page 39 for advice on indoor kennels.)

It may be worth investing in a little DIY here, which can help solve the problem. Get a thin, flat piece of hardboard and buy an ordinary battery-operated door-bell, complete with wire. Fix up the bell outside your bedroom door, running the wire to the back door, to floor level. Attach the bell push towards the edge of the board and connect up the wire. Place the board, bell push side down, on the floor by the back door, if possible under the floor covering. When you put pressure on the board, the bell should ring. When your dog next goes to stand by the back door, asking to go out, he will stand on the board and hey presto! He will have operated the bell, alerting you that he wants to go outside. I have used this with several of my puppies, to great effect.

Sometimes it may just be a matter of altering his feeding times. If he is normally fed his last meal of the day around 6 pm his natural bodily functions will decree that he will want to relieve himself at about 3 am. Try either bringing his last meal forward, or leaving it until much later. Also, to ensure that his bladder is empty before he goes to bed, pick up the water bowl at 5 pm. Obviously, if he has been playing energetically, allow access to the water for a short while to satisfy his thirst, then remove it again.

Only Going to the Toilet in Their Own Garden
There are some dogs who, having grasped the idea of going to the toilet in the garden, seem to think that is the *only* place they can go. You take them out for a walk, but they 'hang on' until they return home. Maturity usually tends to solve this particular snag, but in the meantime it can be quite a problem, especially if you are taking the dog out for the day, or going away on holiday. You must persevere with the training, encouraging him all the time he is outside, giving him the command he has learnt in the garden.

If necessary, stop him going into the garden at all for a few days. On every occasion when he normally wants to go to the toilet, put him on his lead and take him out to the park or wherever, giving him his command and, eventually, nature should take over! This may be time-consuming but it will pay dividends in the end.

In view of the enormous amount of publicity which

has been given to the problem of dogs fouling public areas, it can sometimes be a positive advantage if your dog prefers his own back garden! Do try and be a thoughtful dog owner when you are out exercising your dog. No-one, dog owner or non-dog owner, likes stepping in dog excreta, so always take a few plastic bags with you so that you can clear up after your dog. Plastic bags are not cumbersome and are very simple to use. Just place your hand inside the bag, scoop up the 'deposit', turn the bag inside out using your other hand, seal it and place it in the nearest litter bin. Your hand will not come into contact with anything unpleasant and your dog will not be causing any offence by leaving little 'presents' behind him!

Accidents Caused by Excitement
This seems to be more common with young animals and usually affects bitches more than males. Usually the dog doesn't want or intend to be dirty, but gets so excited that he simply cannot help himself. First of all, DO NOT PUNISH THE DOG, you will only make matters worse, as the dog will become so nervous of your reaction that he will relieve himself through fear. To try and overcome the situation, be very calm when you first greet your dog – not cool, but controlled – and immediately go through to the garden with the dog, where you can greet him properly and any 'accident' will not matter.

Usually they grow out of this problem, but if it persists, it may be something physical and a trip to the vet may be necessary.

Backward Steps
It is quite common for dogs who have previously 'got the idea' of being clean to revert to being unclean again, usually when they are around four to five months old. This generally coincides with them starting to teethe and is only a passing phase. Understanding and patience are required and a few days' repetition of initial

house-training will usually sort the problem out.

Likewise, some bitches forget their house-training just before they start their season. It is basically because their hormones are 'having a sort out' and is only temporary, so do be patient. Emotional upset within the family, moving house, or indeed any change in the normal routine can get the dog's 'wires' crossed temporarily. This especially applies to 'rescue' dogs, who may have undergone quite an emotional trauma and are having difficulty adjusting to a new home and new routine. Do be really patient, treat the dog as you would a young puppy and the problem will soon be solved.

Strange Sights and Sounds
As soon as you bring a new puppy into your home, start accustoming him to as many different sights and sounds as possible. This applies equally to older dogs to whom you have given a home, as you have no way of knowing what might frighten them. Get them used to all the usual domestic noises, such as the washing machine, vacuum cleaner, hairdryer, etc. Deal with any show of fear as it arises, being very calm, patient and loving. As soon as the dog has had all his inoculations, make a point of taking him along roads which have heavy traffic, accustom him to pedestrian crossings, level crossings, etc. Take him across pedestrian bridges and under pedestrian subways. If he shows apprehension at any of these things, don't avoid them, but make a point of taking him to them regularly. For example, if he is showing fear of heavy traffic, take the time to stand on the pavement with him – obviously well back from the edge of the road – talk calmly to him all the time, stroke him and, if necessary, give him the odd titbit. Don't baby him, or try and avoid taking him past any of his 'terrors'. You will only make matters worse. If you are too sympathetic, it will only convince him that there really is something to be frightened of. He needs to get his confidence from you, so adopt a gentle but chivvying

attitude, be kind, give lots of fuss, but don't try to protect him.

If your puppy is still small, don't be tempted to pick him up. Apart from not curing his fear, you could be setting up a situation when he will ask to be carried – easy enough when he only weighs a few pounds, but a full grown Labrador or similar is not so easy to pick up! Likewise, if you have a small dog, which is easy to carry, please don't. However tiny they may be, they are *dogs*, and as such should be treated like dogs, not children.

Make a point of taking the dog to crowded, noisy places. An ideal venue to socialise your dog is the local pub. The combination of crowds of people, juke boxes and fruit machines will all help to make him completely bomb-proof. Of course, another advantage of taking him to the pub is that it gives you a perfect excuse for 'popping down to the local'! Don't forget to take the dog though!

Grooming and Examining Your Puppy
Whatever type of coat your puppy has, you should start by brushing him daily, so that his coat never gets into a tangled or unkempt state. If that happens, grooming could cause the puppy discomfort, which will not aid his acceptance of the procedure. Even when he still has his 'baby' coat, daily gentle brushing will get him used to accepting that this is a normal part of his life. Obviously, at the start you will be using a soft brush, only progressing to a harder brush and comb when the puppy's adult coat has come through.

Whilst you are brushing, you can check your puppy over, firstly so that you can detect any possible problem that may be developing, and also to teach the puppy to stand still and be examined, as he will have to at the vet. Regularly looking at his teeth, ears, feet, tummy and so on, touching and feeling him all over, as the vet might do, will all help in spotting a potential health problem. If you are used to how the dog looks when he is healthy, you will quickly notice when something is amiss. A puppy who accepts having his ears examined, or having his feet picked up and felt, will be more prepared to be examined by the vet, if and when there is a problem. Your puppy may need his toe nails clipping, for example, and if he has never had his feet touched before, such a procedure will be extremely difficult for your vet to perform.

If you have a male puppy, you should check that he is developing properly – his testicles will be held up inside his body to begin with, and will eventually descend by the time he is an adult dog. Very occasionally the testes become retained inside, which will be a matter for your vet to deal with, so you will need to check regularly to ensure that the puppy is maturing as he should.

If you have a female puppy, it is best to let her have at least one season before you have her spayed (see page 175). Bitch puppies come into season any time from five months onwards, and you should know what she looks like around her vaginal area when she *isn't* in season, so that you can spot the difference when she is!

If the idea of checking these basic things is abhorrent to you, then perhaps now is the time to think again about getting a dog! (See also Chapter 12, page 181.)

Cleaning the Dog's Teeth
This should be included in the grooming and examination routine. (See Chapter 12, page 189.)

Leaving the Puppy Alone
All dogs have to be left alone sometimes, and the puppy will have to learn that there will be regular periods when you go out without him. Slowly you will need to acclimatise him to being left, starting with just a few minutes and building up to longer periods over the weeks and months ahead.

To begin with, get the puppy used to being left in one room whilst you are in another, just for a couple of minutes. Yet again, the indoor kennel is invaluable here, enabling you simply to put him into his kennel and close the door, which prevents him from being able to follow you. Leave the room and close the door behind you. You don't have to creep about trying to be quiet – you want the pup just to get used to the idea that he doesn't always follow you.

Within a few days, you should easily be able to leave the puppy alone in one room for at least half an hour. Once you have reached that goal, you can now begin to leave him in that room whilst you go out, to begin with for no longer than fifteen minutes. Always make sure that the puppy has been outside to go to the toilet first, and has suitable toys to amuse him whilst you are out. Again, over a period of a few days, you should be able to build up the period of being left to about one hour.

Ideally, no dog should be left for more than three hours at a time. If you have to leave him for longer periods, you should arrange for someone to come in after a couple of hours, to let the puppy into the garden, and to give the puppy some company for a while.

Leaving Adult Dogs Alone
Hopefully, the adult dog you have brought into your home has already learned that at times he has to remain alone. There are some dogs, though, who have become anxious about being left and will chew and demolish everything they can lay their teeth on, howl or bark, soil indoors and even sometimes self mutilate, the whole time you are out. For these dogs, being left is almost like being punished. They find it particularly stressful as they don't understand what they may have done to receive such treatment from you. Dogs who have already had several homes may be particularly affected by being left. Quite simply, because they have already 'lost' previous owners, when you leave them to go out, they don't know if you're coming back or if they have been deserted once again. When you are at home, the dog may follow you from room to room, even to the bathroom. He may always want to sit at your feet, perhaps with one of his paws on your foot. He may object when

a door is accidentally closed on him. All these are signs that the dog is suffering from what is called 'separation anxiety'.

This problem can be sorted out, although it is a slow process. To begin with, shut the dog in a room on his own for just fifteen seconds. When you put him in the room, be very cool, not cross, but just leave him in there without saying anything. Leave an article of your clothing laying across the bottom of the outside of the door. That way, when he sits and sniffs at the door, he will be able to smell you, which will reassure him. Leave a radio on in the room with him, and an interesting toy to play with. Don't be tempted to try for longer than fifteen seconds to start with.

When he can be left for that length of time without scratching at the door, or barking or howling, start building up the time until you can leave him for ten minutes. You can then start preparing to leave the dog when you go out. Make sure he has had a good walk before you go. Leaving him with a full stomach will encourage the dog to rest. Up until this time, you will have probably found that the dog begins to get worried long before you actually leave him, following you about and initiating contact with you whenever he can. This is because he 'picks up the signals' that you are going out, as your routine is always the same. That routine culminates in you perhaps putting on your coat, or picking up your keys, then giving the dog a cuddle, to reassure him.

What you need to do is completely change your leaving routine, so that the dog cannot pick up on the leaving signals. Reduce contact with the dog at least an hour before you go out. You don't need to be cross with him, just don't talk to or touch him. If he tries to initiate contact with you, ignore him. When it is time to leave, just walk out, saying nothing to the dog. By following this procedure, you are slowly withdrawing from the closeness which has previously been present up until the moment you leave. One minute, the dog has been in warm contact with you, and the next, you're gone, leaving him bereft. By slowly reducing that contact prior to leaving, the act of you going is not nearly so stressful for the dog. When you return, you can greet the dog lovingly as usual – even if you find he has destroyed something whilst you have been out!

If you are cross with him when you come home, he does not know that it is because he has chewed something precious. All he learns is that you are angry when you return, and probably best avoided. The next time you return home, it is likely the dog will be even more stressed, as he will be anticipating your grumpy return. As such, the stress he feels may well culminate in even more damage being done, and thus the circle of destruction continues!

Although all dogs have to be left alone at some stage, I consider three to four hours is the maximum a dog should be left alone – even then not until he is mature and certainly not on a regular, or worse still, day-to-day basis. Dogs are naturally gregarious; they like people's company and if they are left alone for long periods they can become either depressed, or destructive, or both.

Training Classes
Puppy Parties
Because early socialising with a new puppy is so important to his mental development, many vets are now running puppy parties at their surgeries. Puppies who are not yet fully vaccinated, and therefore unable to go outside on the ground yet, can interact with other puppies in the clinical environment of the surgery. Whilst the puppies are interacting with each other, their owners receive basic advice on the training and general care of the puppy. The parties are held outside normal consulting hours, and the floor will have been cleaned with an anti-bacterial and virucidal disinfectant. Bearing in mind that the puppies will not have been exposed to external infection, either from the ground or from contact with other dogs, and having been brought straight from home and returning back there afterwards, the risk

of infection is extremely low. Puppy to puppy cross-infection is possible, so you will be advised, before attending, not to bring your puppy if he is showing any signs of illness, such as diarrhoea, coughing or scratching.

The advantages of early socialisation far outweigh the very slight risk of infection, so, if your veterinary surgeon offers this service, do make the most of the opportunity.

Dog Training Clubs
As a dog trainer and behaviourist, I am obviously going to recommend that you take your puppy, or your older dog, to classes. Nowadays, with more classes catering for puppies from 13 weeks old and upwards, it is invaluable from the point of view of stopping possible problems before they become a learned behaviour. The puppies also learn basic commands such as **sit**, **stay** and **come**, all whilst in the company of other puppies, which is what will be expected of your pup when out on exercise. It is all very well teaching your puppy to be obedient whilst in the confines of your own home, but frequently you will find that all his training is forgotten as soon as the puppy meets another dog outside. Going to classes is also a good way of socialising your pup with other like-minded people, who are unlikely to get upset if your puppy jumps up or licks them.

For the adult dog, classes are a good way to build up the bond between you and the dog, as the dog will be taught to obey you, as the new leader of the pack. You will also be able to get help with any problems that may occur, as the dog settles into his new home.

Most veterinary surgeries have details of where training classes are held. Recommendation is often the best way of picking a training club, as by talking to other dog owners you can find the right class for you. Training methods have changed enormously over the years, and most clubs now teach along the lines of positive reinforcement, that is, praising all the good stuff your dog does whilst ignoring any wrong behaviour as much as possible. Classes which use negative reinforcement, that is, punishing the wrong behaviour, are to be avoided. Dogs do not understand our values, and only by praising all the things we like will they learn what pleases us. To punish them when they make a mistake, when in their mind it is not a mistake but normal dog behaviour, only builds up mistrust in their minds, making future training more difficult.

8

Dogs Being Dogs!

Most of the behaviour which your puppy or adult dog exhibits is simply explained. It is because he is a dog, and that's what dogs do! What you *can* do is to reshape and/or channel these behaviours, in a dog logical way, until they are acceptable to you.

Jumping Up – Puppies

When trying to deter or to 'de-train' a dog from any behaviour, it is important to understand the reason for his exhibiting this behaviour in the first place. All puppies will try to jump up at you, or your visitors. They do this because they want to get close to our faces and particularly our mouths – a food-soliciting behaviour carried over from when dogs were wild. It can also be dominance related – the dog wants to place his paws on you. Initially, when a puppy jumps up at us our reaction teaches him that we like him doing it. How does that happen? One or more of several things occur which confirms in the dog's mind that he is pleasing us. With little puppies especially, we tend to tolerate the jumping up because they are sweet and appealing, and we feel they need our reassurance all the time. We are also sometimes quietly pleased that the puppy wants our attention. Once we get tired of the puppy jumping at us, we start pushing him off and at the same time talking to him, telling him to get off. Either reaction is pleasant for the puppy – he is either being touched, spoken to, or both. Even if you push the puppy off abruptly, they like to play fight quite roughly, so do not see being pushed off as a deterrent, even seeing it as a game. To the dog, his action has provoked a reaction from you that will prompt a repeat of the behaviour, so he will continue to jump up.

So, to stop him jumping up, you have to change the previous rewarding experience for the dog into an *unre-warding* one. IGNORE the dog completely. Don't touch or speak to him. Turn your back on him, folding your arms so they are not accessible for the dog to touch. If he jumps at your back, take a step away from him. Don't acknowledge him in any way all the time he is jumping up at you. When he eventually has four feet on the ground, immediately *go down to his level* and give him a big fuss and a titbit.

Eventually, when you have taught him to sit on command, you can reinforce the control by making him sit as well, but at this stage you simply want him to understand that four feet on the floor get attention, whereas two feet on you does not! If everyone who comes to the house follows the same procedure, the puppy will quickly learn that the way to get attention is to remain on the floor.

Fig. 6. To stop the dog jumping up, ignore him completely.

Jumping up – Adult Dogs

If you have an older dog who is still jumping up, you need to adopt a different approach. Although part of the reason why the dog jumps up is the same, there is also an element of dominance-related behaviour in adult dogs. Height equals status to a dog, and if he can obtain that status at the same time as touching you, the more important he feels. Ignoring the dog is not enough, so as he goes to jump at you, glare at him coldly and say in a loud voice '**GET OFF**', and then turn your back and ignore him. Again, once he has stopped attempting to jump, tell him to sit and reward him – you will be rewarding him for sitting, remember, *not* for not jumping up. If he tries to jump up at your back, take a step or two away from him. As with the puppies, if his actions (jumping up) do not provoke the *re*action he wants, he will cease.

Please do not use the word **down** for this exercise – **down** is later going to mean something else, and you do not want to confuse the dog, or give him a chance to misunderstand.

Finally, it will help if you teach the dog formally to say hello to visitors by always sitting first, being rewarded with a titbit from the visitor. That way you will again reinforce to the dog that the way to get what he wants is to sit. If you use the words 'Say hello' on every occasion when a visitor arrives, you will soon find that he will sit immediately when a visitor appears.

Barking

The dog which barks unnecessarily is a pain to live with and agony to live next door to! Some dogs bark because their guarding instinct is very strong and they feel it necessary to alert you to every little noise. Some bark because they are nervous and the sound of their own barking gives them confidence. Some bark because they like the reaction it provokes in you and some bark simply because they haven't been taught not to. It is quite normal for a dog to bark if someone comes to the door or if he hears a strange noise during the night. Continuing to bark after an acceptable time is what you want to deter.

In most cases, the way to stop a dog barking is to teach him to bark on command! This may sound very strange, but it does work. At the same time as teaching him to bark, you are also teaching him when *not* to bark.

For the dog to learn this exercise, you need to enlist the help of a friend, so that you can set up the situation. You should be sitting relaxing, then your helper, at a pre-arranged time, should come to the door and ring the bell. Your dog will then naturally bark and as he does so, give him the command **speak**. Allow him to bark for five seconds, then command him **quiet**, giving him lots of fuss when he does. Don't attempt to answer the door until the dog is silent. Then go to the door, open it, speak to your friend on the doorstep, as you would a casual caller, then close the door.

Go back and sit down again and after an interval of about ten minutes, repeat the whole process again. Alternate between talking to your friend on the doorstep and inviting him in, to simulate what would sometimes happen, i.e. someone coming to the door, then being invited into the house.

Try to repeat this over a few days, building up the association with the dog that he is allowed to bark for just a few seconds when that doorbell rings, but he must stop when you say so, the door never being opened until he has stopped barking. You are also getting him to associate the sound of your command **speak** with his barking.

Why must the door *never* be opened until he is silent? If you allow him to continue to bark whilst you open the door, he will associate that it is his action of barking which gets the door open, resulting in future problems. If he is the type of dog who imagines there is someone at the door and barks often unnecessarily, the only way you will get him to be quiet is to go and open it. You may even end up in a situation of the dog training you – every time he wants attention, he will bark to provoke you into getting up to answer the door to an imaginary caller.

Having taught him to bark on the command **speak**, you will then be able to get him to bark if ever you feel in a threatening situation – when you're out for a walk, perhaps, and are approached by a suspicious character, or if you should hear a strange noise in the middle of the night. You can also apply the same training if your dog barks every time the telephone rings. Arrange for a friend to telephone you and don't answer until the dog is quiet. On these occasions though, don't practise by giving him the **speak** command, as you don't want him barking every time the phone rings. Simply correct him for barking unnecessarily at the telephone.

Dogs who Bark Because They Like the Reaction it Provokes

Sometimes it is your action in response to the dog barking which can actually make the situation worse. In an attempt to shut the dog up quickly, you tend to rush to answer the door or the telephone and in the process get the dog even more excited. If you think you may be guilty of this, then deliberately do not answer the door, etc., having previously arranged with a friend either to telephone or ring your doorbell. If you show no sign of agitation with the ringing noise, you will take the excitement out of the situation.

You may have fallen into the trap of shouting at the dog each time he barks – or even taken to chasing after him to get him to be quiet. As far as he is concerned, the whole thing turns into a game, at the same time he has learned how to provoke you and get you to lose your temper, thus challenging your authority as pack leader.

He may be the type of dog who simply stands in the garden, head thrown back, barking like crazy and waiting for some reaction from you. If you recognise this situation, indulge in what I call 'negative' training. As it is your reaction which excites and stimulates him, you are going to show no reaction whatsoever. It isn't easy to ignore a barking dog, but you need to give an Oscar-winning performance of complete indifference! Don't speak to him, don't look at him, read the newspaper, pretend to be asleep, show no reaction *at all*. The dog will then probably become curious as to your lack of interest and will come over to you inquiringly. When he does, give him a calm, gentle pat, tell him 'good dog', etc., and carry on reading. As far as he is concerned, it's no fun if he can't get you to react, so he will shut up.

After a few minutes of silence, make a point of going over to him and fuss and play with him. You are thereby conditioning the dog that noise gets no reaction from you, but when he is silent he gets the attention he wants.

The Nervous, Hysterical Barker

If you have the type of dog who rushes out into the garden, barking at unseen terrors, or simply rushes out barking because he likes the sound of his own voice, shock tactics can sometimes work.

Have ready a plastic jug filled with cold water. When he starts his ear-splitting routine, sidle up to him very casually and throw the water over his head. Don't speak as you do it, but praise him like mad the second he stops. Better still, if you can arrange to 'bomb' him with the water from an upstairs window, or from an unobserved position, without him realising where the water has come from, it can be far more effective. Once again, he will have received a most unpleasant reaction to his barking, which should prove quite a deterrent in the future.

This method can also be applied if you have a dog who barks whilst travelling in the car. Substitute for the jug a water pistol or plant spray. When the barking starts, aim the jet of the spray between his eyes, again saying nothing as you do it, but praising like mad when he stops. It is obviously much safer if someone else is driving the car at the time!

Mouthing and Biting – Puppies

All puppies will attempt to mouth and bite their human family. It is perfectly normal behaviour, developed when they are still with their siblings in the litter. The sharp, needle-like teeth, which the puppy has until around 16 to 18 weeks of age, are there for a very good reason – to cause pain, but little damage. The jaw muscles are not so strong at that age and, by play fighting with their litter mates, and later with us, these teeth enable them to cause and feel pain.

When playing with their litter brothers and sisters, they learn that, if they bite too hard, the puppy who has been bitten yelps loudly, and then often refuses to continue playing. Likewise, when they are bitten, they yelp and run away from the biter. Thus they learn that biting too hard hurts and stops the fun – an unrewarding experience. The process continues and they learn to modify the biting whilst playing, until a level is reached which the other puppies can tolerate.

The difference when they attempt to repeat that behaviour with us is that we have to show the puppy that we will not tolerate any level of biting. We should use the already learned response when the puppy attempts either to bite or even simply 'hold' our hand in his mouth. A very sharp scream of 'OUCH', followed immediately by ceasing all contact with the puppy for a few minutes, will prompt the memory learned in the litter. Our 'yelp' will remind him of *his* yelp when he was bitten, and our refusal to play or interact with him will again remind him of how his siblings ceased playing when he bit them.

After the 'time-out' of a couple of minutes, re-establish contact with the puppy. You may find that the pup will attempt to lick you, as a sign of appeasement. If you do not object to the puppy licking you, then as he does so, use the word 'gently', to show the puppy that this is acceptable, and to begin conditioning him to that sound, which will prompt a repeat of the action. You may find that the puppy will simply try to bite again, probably a little softer this time. If he does, repeat the yelp procedure, until you are able to re-establish contact with him without him attempting to open his mouth on you.

Puppies will repeat behaviour they find rewarding, i.e. a game and contact with you. They will cease behaviour that is unrewarding, i.e. mouthing and biting stops the contact.

Mouthing and Biting – Adult Dogs
If you have taken on an adult dog who has not learned properly that biting or mouthing humans is unaccept-able, he will sometimes use such behaviour in an attempt to dominate you, to try and take over as pack leader. If allowed to continue, it may eventually lead to the dog biting seriously, causing damage. Your reaction to this behaviour from an adult dog is very different from that used on a puppy.

Any attempt to take hold of your hand, or clothing, should be met with a loud 'GET OFF', and glaring eye contact. Don't shout or scream, simply adopt the attitude of 'How dare you do that to the boss of the pack?'. DON'T reward him by saying 'Good boy' when he stops. A dog should not be rewarded for stopping behaviour that he shouldn't have been doing in the first place! When the dog has stopped, reinforce your mental dominance by ordering the dog to do something for you, however small. Tell him to sit, or lie down. When he has completed that action for you, you can *then* reward him for compliance, showing him the type of behaviour which you will accept and praise him for.

Do not encourage rough or competitive play with your dog at any time, especially with children. When their play gets too boisterous, this is when the dog can get over-excited and will start to mouth again. It is not that the dog is automatically aggressive – to him it is natural to use his teeth, but unfortunately this can lead to the dog hurting you and in turn ends up with you losing your temper, shouting at the dog and perhaps slapping him, in an attempt to re-gain control. Although seemingly logical to us, the louder and more physical you become, the more the dog gets 'wound up', resulting in him attempting to bite harder, possibly ending up doing serious damage.

Chase type games should always be avoided, as this encourages the dog to jump and bite, either at clothes or hands. Similarly, games with tug type toys should also be avoided. These types of games place the dog in a competitive situation – if he wins the 'trophy' it will reinforce his opinion that he is top dog and will hinder future training. If you win, through brute force, it will make the dog even more determined to use his stronger qualities, i.e. his teeth, in any future confrontation over perceived trophies.

It is instinctive for a dog to try to win in a confrontation – that is how he survived in the wild. What we have to do is to make the 'losing' as pleasant and as non-confrontational as possible. When he tries to chew you or your clothes, give him something he *can* chew, such as a toy. As previously mentioned, try not to get involved in situations where one of you has to physically win. For example, don't be tempted into chasing after the dog if he steals something, as this again will become a win or lose situation. (See also *Dogs who Steal*, page 101.) Encourage him to give up what he has stolen by offering an alternative that he *is* allowed, or better still in this case, offer him food as a reward – food is, after all, his number one priority.

Remember that for a dog to use his teeth to 'hold' things, be it us or our clothes, is all quite natural for the dog and is not wrong – it is simply that it is not acceptable to us and we have to make it clear to the dog that we will neither encourage such behaviour nor allow it to develop.

Chewing and Destructiveness
If you follow the earlier suggestion of having an indoor kennel for your puppy, you will find that you will not

have much of a problem in the chewing department. Providing the puppy with something appropriate to chew on when he is teething will also deter him from chewing on furniture and so on. Occasionally, the dog may go through a second chewing stage, between six to nine months, as the new adult teeth are settling into the jaw bone. Again, suitable chew toys, or better still a raw bone, given at that time will save your furniture.

Lack of exercise and mental stimulation can also create the need for the dog to relieve the boredom by chewing. Most of the damage done by chewing usually occurs whilst you are out of the house. Please remember that chewing or destroying your home is NOT done out of spite. The act of chewing is self-rewarding, either by easing the aching teeth, chewing something which smells of you if the puppy is lonely, or employing the 'killing' instinct by shredding your settee! Imagine how shocked and confused the dog becomes when you return home. He has been indulging in a self-rewarding and pacifying activity, with no thought of upsetting you. Then you come in and are very angry. This in turn can lead to chewing through anxiety, and so the whole procedure becomes a vicious circle.

By ensuring that the puppy is safely contained away from the furniture, has suitable toys to stimulate his brain, has something he can demolish, and has been played with and/or exercised before being left alone, you will be able to control this aspect of your puppy's development to within an acceptable level. (See also page 101.)

Howling and Chewing
Sometimes the silence of an empty house can distress the dog and may start him howling or barking. Sometimes, because of the silence, dogs can hear noises outside more easily, thereby provoking them into barking. Try leaving the radio on when you go out, as the sound of human voices may soothe the distressed dog and mask the external sounds for the barking dog.

Some dogs learn to be very destructive when they are left alone and young puppies, particularly, like to chew, especially when they are losing their baby teeth. In this instance, leave them something they *can* chew which is not going to matter. I have found that a pile of empty cardboard boxes, the sort you can get from the supermarket, provide a dog with endless amusement, as they can demolish them beautifully! Of course, you must remove any staples or wire first.

By leaving the boxes for him to chew, you are getting two distinct benefits. Firstly, he is not damaging the furniture or the carpets and all you have to clear up when you return are pieces of cardboard. Secondly, you will not inadvertently be teaching him to chew anything precious, as you would if you gave him an old slipper or shoe to play with. If you do actually give him an old shoe to demolish, you can hardly be surprised when he chews up your best pair – how is he supposed to know the difference between old ones and new ones?

For puppies who are teething, I have found that an old saucepan or frying pan comes in useful – and no, not for hitting him with! When he's teething, he wants something cold and hard with which he can ease his painful gums, so you can see that such an article is ideal. Obviously, make sure there are no sharp edges or loose screws on which he could harm himself and don't use the non-stick variety, as this could poison him. One word of warning here – if he tries to carry it around in his mouth, watch out for your shins, as a clout from a metal pan really hurts – and I speak from very painful experience!

Dogs who Steal
It is quite natural for a dog to take things in his mouth – after all, he doesn't have hands! Unfortunately, it is often the owners who inadvertently teach their dogs to steal. A fairly typical reaction to seeing your dog wandering around with your best pair of socks in his mouth, is to chase after him and shout at him to leave

101

them. He runs away and it turns firstly into a game and secondly into a way of challenging your authority and getting you to lose your temper. This all culminates in him stealing at every opportunity.

What you *should* do is to encourage him to bring whatever he has in his mouth to you, by praising him and telling him what a clever dog he is, saying 'Good boy, come and bring it here.' When he does come up, all pleased with himself, reward him and tell him to **give**, holding your hands level with his mouth and taking the article as he opens his mouth. As you are going to be ever so nice when he brings it to you, he will enjoy your reaction so much that he will not want to run away. He may even end up actively seeking things out to bring to you.

You will probably end up with the sofa piled high with socks, clothes, shoes, slippers, shopping bags, etc., but at least they will not have been hidden or destroyed. He will have learned a valuable lesson in what pleases you, plus you will have the added bonus of laying down the groundwork for the retrieve exercise. Retrieving is not necessary for the average pet to learn, but if you want to do obedience competitively later on, you will have already done some basic training towards it.

Car Travel and Travel Sickness

Cars are now an integral part of our lives and as such will also become a necessary part of your dog's routine. Many dogs develop a fear of car travel and become sick during the journey. Unfortunately we as dog owners inadvertently contribute towards this.

Usually the very first experience a dog has with a car is when you collect him from the place where he was bred. The trauma of leaving his mum, brothers and sisters, plus the people he has become used to, is compounded by being put into a moving machine, possibly for several hours. The car thus becomes an upsetting place, associated with being taken away from his first family.

Then, he settles in with you and more than likely his very next trip in the car is to the vet for a check-up and his first inoculations, again compounding his opinion that cars are most unpleasant places to be, this time associated with having an injection. The car has turned into a monster and his dislike of it increases. Fortunately, most dogs do grow out of this phobia as they mature, but some retain their fear.

To change the dog's attitude about the car, make sure that pleasant things happen there – for a week or two feed him one of his daily meals in the car, whilst it is parked outside. Take the time every day and go and sit with him in the car, without the engine running. Have the car radio on and, assuming that he is not showing fear or misapprehension, spend the time talking to and stroking him. If he is shaking, whining or showing any fearful behaviour, *do not initiate or allow any contact.* Touching or talking to the dog whilst he is exhibiting such behaviour will simply re-affirm in his mind that such behaviour is appropriate in that situation, as you are rewarding him for it. Only reward (by touching and talking) behaviour that is non-fearful.

Even before he can go out on the ground and mix with other dogs, take him out for short rides in the car to visit friends or family who will make a fuss of him. If he is prone to being sick, make sure that initially he always travels with an empty stomach.

Dogs will usually travel better in the car if they are confined in one area. If you have an estate car you can buy purpose-made cages which will fit in the rear of the car. With a saloon car, either tie the lead to a strong part of the inside of the car (not the door handle!), or buy a proper dog safety harness, which can be attached securely to the existing car seatbelt, preventing the dog from charging about in the car and, just as importantly, protecting the dog and the front seat passenger in the event of a traffic accident.

Fig. 7. A safety harness prevents your dog from charging about the car.

Mounting – Puppies

Please don't be horrified if your puppy of just a couple of months old attempts to mount you or the children! Both male and female puppies experiment by mounting, either each other or a human. It does not mean that the puppy is perverted. Gently guide the puppy away, and distract him or her with a toy. Sometimes it may be a sign that the puppy is trying to be dominant, but again this should be dealt with in the same way – gentle distraction. If you play down the behaviour, it will cease to be rewarding for the puppy and he or she will grow out of it before reaching adulthood.

Mounting – Adult Dogs

Adult dogs who try to mount are nearly always trying to dominate their human family. Castration for the males, and spaying for the females, will usually sort this problem out, along with some remedial rank re-structuring. (See page 74.)

104

Dogs who Eat Droppings

Almost without exception, when a dog eats his own waste matter, or indeed that of another animal, the owner is appalled and revolted, thinking perhaps that he has a perverted dog on his hands.

The correct term for this practice is coprophagia and not only is it common, it is also normal! It is not a sign of illness and depravity. It is a normal part of the food gathering process. Bearing in mind that your dog is a carnivore, in the wild state he would kill and eat whole prey, including any faecal matter in the bowels of the animal he was eating. The faeces are a rich source of essential enzymes and micro-organisms, and once these elements reach the stomach of the dog, the enzymes aid the digestive processes. The live micro-organisms are killed when they reach the stomach and their fats, proteins, vitamins, etc., are then absorbed by the dog.

Dogs fed on an artificial diet are more likely to eat their own droppings, plus the droppings of other animals. Dogs fed on a natural diet rarely eat their own droppings, as the waste eliminated from a natural diet is simply powdered bone, and has little nutritional value. They may still eat other animal droppings.

Bearing in mind that the dog needs the elements contained in the faeces, you could feed your dog a bowl of animal droppings a couple of times a week! However, a much better way to give your dog the enzymes and probiotics he needs is to give him yoghurt, cottage cheese and eggs. (See Chapter 6, Feeding Your Dog.)

He may still like to eat the natural source sometimes – remember, it's normal! You may also notice that your dog likes to eat soil. That is for the same reasons as eating droppings: he will gain important elements and nutrients from soil, so don't worry about it.

Rolling

Rolling in animal droppings, or indeed other foul smelling substances, is another example of how our dogs unwittingly offend us. We think of it as dirty, disgusting behaviour. To a dog though, it is a normal, instinctive part of his canine personality.

One of the most commonly accepted reasons for this behaviour is that, in dog language, the stronger and more pungent he smells, the more superior he appears to another dog. This desire to smell more powerful than other dogs reverts back to when dogs were wild creatures running in packs. The pack leader would wish to impress on his subordinates that he was still top dog. Or perhaps a dog lower in the pecking order would attempt to challenge the pack leader, so to give him added courage, he would first roll in strong smelling animal droppings.

Although our pet dogs have been domesticated for centuries, the desire and instinct to cover themselves in, to us, evil smells is still very strong, even though they may not know why they are doing it. It could occur because you are still having a tussle with your dog as to who is boss, so the dog reverts to his instinctive behaviour in an attempt to impress you.

Our reaction to our smelly dogs is firstly to reject them, not wanting them to get near us and secondly, to bath them as soon as possible to get rid of the smell. This can in turn merely heighten the desire for the dog to repeat his rolling actions as soon as he gets the chance.

If this behaviour is really causing you a problem, you can purchase a special collar which emits an odour (offensive to the dog), when activated at the appropriate time by a hand-held remote control. (See Appendix for stockist.)

9

Training

You will obviously need to teach your dog the basic obedience required to ensure that he doesn't cause a nuisance to other people, is controlled enough to run freely and safely when out on exercise, and is a pleasure to own.

Hopefully, you will be taking him to classes to continue his formal education, where you can get help in the art of getting him to walk nicely on a lead, sitting and lying down on command, staying when told and coming when called, all in the company of other dogs and their owners. More advanced training is available (see *Obedience Competitions*, page 154), but in terms of the control you will need for a family pet, the following advice should enable you to have a happy and controlled dog.

How to Use the Collar and Lead
The lead and collar are used as a legal requirement and to ensure your dog is with you when you train him! But don't rely on them alone to keep your dog with you. If you simply 'hang on' to him to prevent him either pulling you or wandering off he will just pull even more. As soon as you apply a pulling pressure on the collar, it will make him fight the pressure and try to pull away.

Although you must not rely on the lead to control your dog there should never be a time when you take him out of the house or garden without being attached to you, via the lead, however well-trained he eventually becomes. Apart from being an offence to have your dog off a lead on a main road, it is stupid and potentially very dangerous to allow him to walk free on *any* road. There is always a chance that he could be startled into doing something unpredictable, or be frightened into dashing into the road. As well as risking his life, he could endanger the lives of other animals, or worse, other humans.

If, like me, you are a car driver, you may well have experienced the dilemma of seeing a dog walking along off the lead, with the owner several yards away. You have your foot hovering over the brake pedal, wondering if the dog is about to dash into the road. Just as dangerous is the dog being walked along the pavement on a long extending lead. As the driver of a potentially lethal machine, you may well be put into the position of swerving or braking to avoid the dog, and in the process hit some innocent pedestrian, or at the very least damage someone else's property. Dog owners are now held responsible for any damage their dogs cause, even indirectly, and it could be a very expensive lesson to learn, both for the owner's pocket and his conscience.

Tones of Voice and Visual Signals
As your voice is one of the most important training aids you are going to use, do remember that your dog does not understand the English language. He hears 'sounds' not words, so in theory you can use any word you choose to fit any action, as long as you are consistent. However, it is more realistic for us to use a word that makes sense to us, so we use the word **sit** to get the dog to sit, etc. The tone of the word must be decisive. You don't need to bellow like a sergeant-major, but your voice should convey determination and authority, with you 'telling' your dog, rather than 'asking' him. Each command must also sound different for each separate action.

After each command you will be rewarding your dog, with titbits initially, plus lots of excited, loving sounds, such as 'Good dog', 'Super dog', 'Clever dog', etc., all said in a really happy voice. *Show* him with your hands that you are pleased with him, stroke him lovingly, play with him, let him see that his action of compliance has really pleased you. Praise and reward are *vital* to his learning, so every effort, however small, must be encouraged.

Some exercises will eventually lead to your controlling your dog when he is some distance away from you, so you will be teaching a visual command as well as a verbal one. If you only train with verbal commands you could, for example, have quite a problem getting your dog back to you when he is 200 yards away and the wind is blowing your voice back in the opposite direction. Or suppose you lose your voice – does that mean you also lose control over your dog? Some dogs become deaf as they grow old. Must that mean he can then do as he pleases, because he can no longer hear you?

By giving him audible and visual signals, he has an even better chance of understanding what you want him to do, so that you are not totally dependent on the lead for control.

Sitting on Command
Verbal Command – Dog's name and **sit**.
Visual Signal – Right hand raising up in front of dog's nose.

This is usually the very first exercise that we teach our dogs and is what I describe in my classes as 'gears in neutral, handbrake on'! In other words, the *sit* tends to be used to get the dog's attention before something else happens, i.e. sitting before being petted by visitors, sitting before being fed, or sitting before having the lead put on, or taken off. Most owners manage to teach the dog to sit for a few moments before he gets up of his own accord, but what you want to achieve is the dog sitting *until he is told he can move*.

To begin teaching the *sit*, you don't need to have the dog on a lead, and it doesn't matter if the dog is in front of you or by your side. What is crucial is titbits! Many people seem to think that if you use titbits for training, the dog will never do anything without them, but here we will use titbits as an initial 'lure', whilst at the same time teaching the dog a voice signal and a hand signal which are going to mean 'sit'. Eventually the titbits will be phased right down, only being given occasionally, but to start with you will be using them all the time.

Again, many people would begin to teach the dog to sit by saying the word **sit**, at the same time pushing down on the dog's rump, until he sits. There is a better way! You want the dog to work out what he has to do to get the titbit. In other words, he has to use his brain. If he uses his brain, rather than being pushed or shoved into a position, he will *remember*.

Have plenty of titbits in your pocket, with one or two in your hand. With the palm of your hand facing *upwards*, and holding a titbit between your first three fingers and thumb, 'waft' the titbit in front of the dog's nose, then straight up about three inches directly above his nose, and hold it there. Say nothing. He may just stand there, trying to work out what it is he has to do. He may offer several different 'behaviours' in an attempt to get the titbit. He may bark – ignore it. He may attempt to jump up at your hand – just lower your hand to under the dog's head momentarily and he will stop jumping.

The mere fact that the dog can smell the titbit will make him tip his nose up towards it. As his nose tips up, his back end will dip down and he will sit. As he sits, say the words, 'Good **sit**', dropping your hand to the level of his mouth and offer him the titbit, *without letting go of it*. Let him nibble on it whilst you are still holding it, all the time saying, 'What a good **sit**, clever **sit**', and continue to reward the dog all the time he remains sitting.

You should continue to re-enforce the sound of **sit** all the time he is sitting – building up a sound to go with his action, so that he will learn the command. Keep him in the sit position, allowing him to nibble on the titbit, for about five seconds, then, as you release the titbit

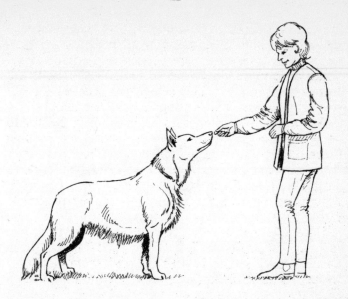

Fig. 8. *Sit* – dog standing, hand holding titbit level with dog's nose.

completely, say, '**That'll do**', and allow the dog to move. You will find that once the titbit has been handed over, the dog will move almost immediately. By using the *That'll do* command, you will teach the dog that, as those words are said, he can move.

If the dog attempts to move from the sit whilst he is still nibbling on the titbit you are holding, just move your hand up slightly, then reposition it just above the dog's nose, as you did initially, and he will sit again.

Once he is sitting immediately your hand goes up in front of his nose, you can start to use the command of **sit** before he sits – in other words, giving him the command to do the action. You will find that the dog will 'pick up' on the hand signal too – as your hand raises, so he will start to sit. He is therefore learning both signals – voice and hand – which is very useful if the dog's hearing deteriorates when he is older, as you

Fig. 9. *Sit* - dog sitting in front of handler, getting titbit.

will still be able to 'tell' him to sit with your hand, even if he can't hear your voice. It's also useful if you lose your voice too!

As soon as you have him sitting every time, off the lead, now go to the next stage, sitting beside your left leg, on the lead. Guide him gently beside your leg, using the titbit, held as previously described, to encourage him to the correct position. Hold the lead in whichever hand feels more comfortable to you, titbit in right hand, and make sure that you are not putting any pressure, via the lead, onto the collar. Now he is beside you, you will need to position your right arm across your body, so that your hand is held just in front of, and slightly above the dog's head. Try to imagine the position your right arm would be in if it were in a sling, and you'll have it in the right place! (Fig. 10.)

Now take one step forward, with the dog, stop and

Fig. 10. *Sit* – dog sitting on handler's left, handler's right arm across body, giving dog titbit.

tell him to **sit**, raising your right hand slightly as you stop. He will sit! Give him the titbit, praise, making sure he doesn't get up, keep him there for a couple of seconds, then break off and play. Repeat this several times, until you can go forward one step, stop, sit, praise, continue for another step, etc., for at least five steps.

You may find that as you stop each time, the dog will sit but slightly creeps around to get in front of you, swinging his rear end out. If this is the case, rather than walking in a straight line, make each step into a very gentle left-hand curve, so that you are *slightly* turning into your dog on each step. Another way of stopping this type of problem is to walk beside a straight wall, with the dog between you and the wall, starting with the dog literally touching the wall. This will physically prevent the dog from swinging around.

If he is coming too far forward, it is probably because

you are holding the titbit out a bit too far. Bringing your arm in closer to your body should stop this happening.

You have now taught your dog to sit each and every time you say so, whether he is on or off lead, and whether he is in front of you (off lead) or beside you (on or off lead). As an additional bonus, you have also made a gentle start on teaching heelwork (see page 144), plus you have started to condition him that each time you stop, he is to sit. Now you can teach him to sit and *stay*.

Sitting and Staying

Verbal Command for *stay* – **stay** (don't use dog's name).
Visual Signal for *stay* – Right hand, palm open towards dog, in front of dog's nose.

The command to *stay* should be used when you want the dog to remain still in a position whilst you move, and to stay in that position *until you return to him* and give him permission to move.

As an example, you may want the dog to accompany you to the front door when a stranger calls. You certainly will not want the dog to rush through the door, possibly getting onto the road, nor do you want him to move forward to greet the person at the door – you simply wish him to remain in one position, under control, whilst you deal with the caller.

Another good reason for teaching *stay* is in the case of domestic accidents, like broken glass on the floor. You don't want to step over the glass to remove the dog to another room, and you certainly don't want the dog walking through the glass to get to you.

Start by sitting the dog beside you, attached to his lead, as if you were about to set off walking. Make sure that you do not put any tension on the lead. Say the word **stay** calmly but firmly. If the dog is sitting on your left side, slowly move your right foot forward, as though you were going to take a step forward, then place it back by your left foot. (If the dog is sitting on your right, you would move your left foot.) You want to take two or three of these 'dummy' steps forward, calmly saying **stay**, without the dog moving. By moving the foot furthest away from the dog, he is less likely to get up immediately. If he should try and move, either by lying down or moving forward, calmly put him back in the original position and start again.

When you can move your foot five times without him attempting to follow, take one step forward and turn and face him. Keep repeating the *stay* command gently, at the same time verbally rewarding him, saying, 'Good **stay**'. Don't sound too excited, or he will get up, and use a gentle tone. Try and aim for about five seconds in front, and then, still saying, 'Good **stay**', step back to the side. Don't let him move immediately you return to the side, or he may start to associate your return with him getting up. Keep him staying at your side for at least three seconds, stroking him calmly on the top of his

Fig. 11. *Sit, Stay* – dog sitting on left, handler moving right foot.

head. Then gently take a step *backwards*, at the same time telling the dog, '**That'll do**', and turning his head slightly towards you, encouraging the dog to move backwards as you do, and releasing him from the exercise. You are aiming at conditioning the dog so that he only ever moves backwards after completing a stay, thus discouraging him from breaking the stay by moving forwards.

Don't be in too much of a hurry to let go of the lead, or get further away. Over about a week, you should aim for leaving the dog for fifteen seconds, with you standing in front, the length of the lead away, but still loosely holding onto it. Slowly, over several weeks, you can build up both the time and the distance, but you want to aim at stability before distance.

When you have reached the position of him sitting and staying for the required time and distance, start to leave him at different angles, i.e. step behind him instead of in front, or step out sideways. Walk around your dog whilst he is sitting. All these things will add to the stability of the exercise.

Do's and Don'ts
When teaching the exercise on the lead, make sure that when you step in front of your dog you don't put any tension or movement on the lead. Obviously, if you do, the dog is likely to get up, as he will interpret the lead movement as a signal for *him* to move.

Don't use the dog's name when you are standing in front of him – again, he associates his name with movement, and may get up. You *can* talk to him to reassure him that he is doing it right, but just avoid using his name.

Don't stare into your dog's eyes when you are standing in front of him. A direct stare could also encourage him to get up – look at a point between his ears, that way you can still watch him without having eye contact.

If the dog moves, don't punish him! Gently 'chide' him, i.e. say, 'Silly dog', etc., and start again. If you punish him for moving, it will make him uneasy about the whole exercise, and you want him to feel happy about staying, rather than tense.

Do make it clear that by staying, he is pleasing you. Tell him softly what a clever dog he is – not in a loud, excited voice, which may encourage him to move, but rather in a gentle, loving voice.

Lying Down
Verbal Command – Dog's name and **down**.

Visual Signal – Right hand level with dog's head, then lower hand to the floor.

To lie down for you is an act of submission on the part of the dog, so you should try to make it as pleasant as possible, bearing in mind that the dog could see it as 'losing face'. You may have noticed that when two strange dogs confront one another, one dog will sometimes lie down, often rolling right over on his back. This is a submissive act, showing the standing dog that the lying down dog recognises him as being dominant, and that the submissive dog poses no threat to him. Each time your dog lies down for you, your dog is sending you a similar message.

Before you even begin teaching him on the lead to lie down, you can start to condition him to the sound of the command, i.e. **down**, by cheating a little. Every time you see your dog about to lie down naturally, as he starts to 'bend' give him the *down* command, and praise him. Once he's down, repeat the verbal command again, saying, 'What a good **down**, clever dog, good **down**', etc. He will quickly associate his, albeit voluntary, act of lying down with praise and reward from you, together with the sound of the command **down**.

In the same way that you teach the *sit*, the *down* is taught with titbits initially, backed up with a hand signal. To begin with, do not say anything until the dog offers the correct behaviour, that is, he lies down. The dog should be sitting before you start the exercise – eventually you will be able to get him to lie down from the standing position, but to begin with it is easier for both of you if he is sitting. Again, you need two or three titbits in your hand, held slightly under your fingers with your thumb, but this time you hold your hand *palm downwards*. Start with your hand adjacent to and immediately in front of the dog's nose, and take your hand directly down until your hand is resting on the floor, ending up in the middle of the space between the dog's front paws and directly below his nose. Keep your hand still. The dog will probably just tip his head downwards to begin with, without lying down. He may scratch at your hand with his paw. Ignore it, and if necessary slightly move your hand to avoid his paw. He may stand up from the sit position – if he does, simply repeat the **sit**, reward him verbally for sitting, but don't give him a titbit for sitting this time, as on this occasion he has to earn the titbit by lying down. He may bark – ignore it. Don't be tempted into saying anything. You want the dog to work out for himself just what he has to do to get the titbit. Some dogs seem to get the hang of this very quickly, and will lie down within a few seconds. Others may take several minutes for the penny to drop. You will know when the dog is getting an inkling of what to do when he not only tips his head down to your hand, but he slightly bends his front legs. When this happens, *slowly* slide your hand about four to six inches out from his nose, without moving your hand from the floor. As his nose follows your hand, so his shoulders will bend and he will be lying down. The second his shoulders touch the floor, give him access to the titbit *without letting go* and tell him, 'Good **down**, clever **down**.' Allow him to nibble on the titbit for a few seconds whilst he is still lying down, then give it to him, saying, '**That'll do**', and allowing him to move.

You then progress to showing the dog where and when you want him to lie down. Put him on his lead, and with him sitting beside your left leg, hold the lead in your left hand. Have a titbit in your right hand. Go down on one knee beside the dog. Hold the titbit between your thumb and first two fingers, and 'show' the dog the titbit, an inch or so in front of and level with his nose. Then take the titbit, still in your fingers, straight down to the floor and keep it still. (Fig. 12.) Make sure that your hand is palm downwards, with the titbit covered by your fingers. *Do not say anything*. The dog's head will naturally follow the titbit to the floor. Once his nose is level with your hand on the floor, carefully slide your hand about two inches straight out level with his nose. *Do not say anything*. After a few seconds the dog will 'drop' his front legs and lie down. As he does so, and *whilst he is still lying down*, give him the titbit and tell him, 'Good **down**, clever dog', etc. (Fig. 13.) Keep him there for a few seconds by continuing to praise him and if necessary give him another titbit, then tell him, '**That'll do**', stand up and encourage him to get up too.

After repeating the above a few more times, only saying the *down* command once he is lying down, you can now start using the *down* sound as you lower the

Fig. 12. *Down* – dog sitting by left leg, with handler kneeling by dog, hand holding titbit going to floor.

titbit to the floor. Very quickly he will start to follow your hand and your voice command. Say the command nicely but with a gentle authority – don't bellow, and don't make it sound like a punishment.

Possible Problems
One of the commonest problems when you start teaching the *down* command is that as the dog's head follows the titbit to the floor, his back end comes up. Don't continue trying to get the dog to lie down from the standing position. Give him the *sit* command, and start again. Eventually, once the command has been learnt, he will happily lie down from standing up, but to begin with it is a hard concept for him to take in.

HAVING AN UNPLEASANT ASSOCIATION WITH BEING TOLD TO LIE DOWN
Perhaps in the past the dog has been told to lie down in a punishing tone, or even been physically forced to lie down, either by being pushed, or worse still, having his front legs pulled out to make him drop to the ground.

Fig. 13. *Down* – dog lying down, handler giving titbit.

He will by now have built up an unpleasant association with being told to lie down. If that is the case, I would suggest that you choose another sound command – perhaps the word **flat** or **floor**. Changing the command sound will take away the initial unpleasant connection and may help to stop the dog from 'stiffening up' when he hears the command. You will need to be on a non-carpeted surface, either lino or floorboards. Kneel down beside the dog, and cuddle him into your left side. Be prepared to be very patient, if necessary cuddling him up to you for several minutes. When he relaxes, you will find he will be leaning into your body. With the titbit positioned as before, slowly and gently slide your left leg back, and as you do so the dog will slide gently and gracefully to the floor. Give him praise and the titbit immediately, cuddle him, tickle his tummy, etc. Keep repeating the command you have chosen, saying, 'Good **floor**, clever dog, what a good **floor**.' Anyone who doesn't realise what is happening will of course think you are truly mad, telling the floor how good it is, but *you* know what you are doing, and remember, it's not the word the dog is learning, it's the *sound*.

Down, Stay

Verbal Command – Dog's name and **down, stay**.

Visual Signal – Left hand, palm open facing dog, in front of dog's nose.

Once your dog has learnt to lie down when you say so, the next stage is for him to remain down, whilst you stand up, and eventually walk away. Don't attempt to teach the *stay* until you know your dog understands the *down* and is comfortable in that position, rather than attempting to 'spring' back up. The need to teach him to lie down and stay down are the same as previously mentioned in the *sit and stay*, plus it gives the dog another 'string to his bow'.

Having told him to lie down, with you kneeling by his side, and holding the lead in your right hand, deliver the verbal and visual signals calmly, and start to stand up. Take care not to put any pressure on the collar, via the lead, as you stand up. (Fig. 14.) Any movement of the lead could result in your dog mis-interpreting that movement as a signal for him to get up. If he should attempt to follow you, repeat the *down, stay* command, in a gentle but firm voice. Once you are standing, remain there for five seconds, then kneel back down to your dog, saying, 'Good down **stay**', etc., in a loving tone, then after a couple of seconds, release with the *That'll do* command, and reward.

Repeat this several times, until he is perfectly relaxed about you getting up whilst he stays down. Then progress to the next stage, which you do in exactly the same way as you taught the *sit, stay*, moving your right foot first, as if to take a step, etc. The obvious difference is that you say **down**, *stay*.

The routine differs from the *sit, stay*, when you return to the side of your dog. Having waited a couple of

Fig. 14. *Down, Stay* – the visual signal.

seconds at the side, *go down to his level* to give him a gentle reward, and then release him from the stay by saying, 'That'll do', and allowing him to get up.

If he only gets the reward in the down position, he will not anticipate the reward by jumping up.

Follow the same teaching pattern as you did for the *sit, stay*, over a period of seven days, making your ultimate aim a one minute down, stay, 4–6 feet away.

Again, as with the *sit, stay*, when you reach the position of him staying down whilst you stand a few feet in front of him, start leaving him at different angles, i.e. step behind him, rather than in front, or step out sideways. Start walking around your dog whilst he is staying down. All these things will add to the stability of the *stay* exercise.

A final DON'T. Please never use the *down, stay* as a form of punishment, e.g. 'Go to your basket and stay down.' You want him to enjoy staying down, but if he relates it to being in your bad books, he will start to break the stay, as he will feel uneasy and unhappy in that position, associating it with being in the wrong.

The 'Quick' Down Stay

Having taught your dog to lie down and stay, it can be very useful if you can get your dog to 'drop' instantly and stay. From a control point of view, if the dog ever gets over excited, perhaps during a play session, it can be a very effective stop switch. In an emergency situation, a dog that will drop and stay instantly is much safer than one who is careering about, perhaps in the traffic.

You can teach the *quick down* as a game, either using a toy or a bumper titbit. If your dog likes playing with toys, select his favourite one, and keep it just for this exercise. If toys don't hold much interest for him, have some special titbits in your hand. Have your dog on his lead, and start getting him excited with the toy (or titbit), just keeping it out of his reach and gently 'goading' him with it. Say 'What's this?' and 'What have

I got, do you want it?', all the time twisting and turning round in a tight circle, just keeping it away from him. After about 10–15 seconds, take your hand with the toy or titbit, straight down to the floor, as in the visual *down* signal, and give the verbal **down** command. Your dog will probably 'pounce' downwards onto the reward. Refrain from giving it to him for a couple of seconds, repeating over and over, 'Good **down**, clever dog, good **down**', etc., then let him have the reward. Very quickly he will learn that by 'throwing' himself down, he gets the treat or the toy. If using a toy, let him play with it for a few seconds; if using titbits, give him another couple, then repeat the whole exercise.

To reinforce this exercise further, make him do a *quick down* before you put his lead on when taking him for a walk. If he builds up a pleasant association with the *quick down*, i.e. food, or a toy, or going out, he will always be ready to comply.

Settle
Having taught your dog to sit and lie down beside you, it is a fairly easy step to command your dog to go and **settle**, away from you. **Settle** means, 'That's enough, go and be a good dog and leave me in peace!' It doesn't mean, 'Go and sit' or 'Go and lie'; it just means, 'Go and *be*'. I'm sure you can think of an occasion when you are sitting, perhaps watching television and, after giving your dog a cuddle, you want him to go away and settle, rather than be in your face. Or, after a visitor has arrived, and you want to entertain your guest, you don't want the dog under your feet.

When you decide that it's time for him to go and settle, stop touching him and say, gently but firmly, 'That's enough, go **settle**.' If you reduce all contact, you will find that after a few seconds the dog will walk away from you, choosing where to settle, and relax. As he does so, say softly, 'Good dog.' If you say the praise too excitedly, it will encourage him to come back to your side for more attention. If you repeat that over a period of a few days, you will eventually be able just to say, 'Go **settle**', and he will 'put himself away' quite happily.

Remaining in a Position

Having taught your dog to stay, either in the *sit* or *down*, you can teach him to *wait*. It means something different from the *stay*, so it is vital not to confuse the dog between the two.

Wait

Verbal Command – Dog's name and **wait**.

Visual Signal – One sweep of the left arm, starting from the side of your left leg, over in front of the dog's face – like the pendulum swing of a clock. For some dogs the visual signal can actually encourage them to move, so if you find that happens with your dog, dispense with the hand signal.

This command will teach the dog that it is not appropriate to move forward until he is called, for example when you want to let him out of the car. It would obviously be very unsafe simply to open the car door and allow him to jump out immediately, possibly when the car is parked on a busy road.

Having taught your dog that **stay** means, 'Stay where I tell you until I come back to you', you now need to teach him that **wait** means, 'Wait where I tell you until I give you further commands.' For example, **wait** whilst the door is opened before he jumps out of the car; **wait** whilst the front door is opened properly, rather than trying to push through it half opened; **wait** while you put his dinner on the floor, etc.

A word of caution before you start. Please don't practise the *stay* and *wait* exercises one after the other. You don't want to give your dog any chance of becoming confused. Even though the command is different, at the beginning there is a risk that he may try and anticipate your wishes.

To begin, start with the dog in the normal position, beside your left leg. Remember to leave him right foot

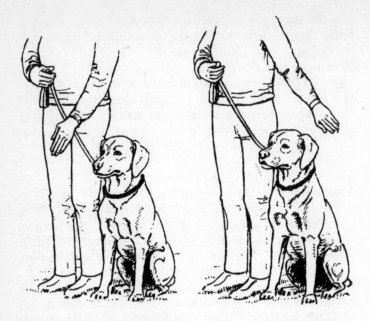

Fig. 15. *Wait* – the hand signal.

first, give him the verbal and visual *wait* commands and step to the front of him. Remain there for a couple of seconds, then repeat the verbal command and back away from him, until you are at the end of the lead (Fig. 16). Stand still and call him to you, rewarding him as he comes.

If he should move before you call, correct him very gently by putting him back on the exact spot again. Don't be too harsh with the correction, as, if you over correct, it may put him off moving and make him hesitant when you call him next time. All the time he remains sitting and waiting, tell him gently what a good dog he is – don't get too excited at this stage, otherwise again it may encourage him to move before you want him to.

By telling him gently that he is good for waiting, he

Fig. 16. Dog waiting.

will understand quicker what he is supposed to be doing. Repeat this two or three times over a couple of days and then start incorporating the *wait* command whenever the situation is appropriate. Getting out of the car is usually where this exercise is most beneficial – there are few things worse, or potentially more dangerous, than a dog which leaps out of the car the instant the door is open. By teaching him the *wait* exercise properly, you will be able to open the car door and know he will not move until you tell him so.

Practise further by putting the dog in the car whilst it is parked outside your house, or if your road is a busy one, drive to somewhere nice and quiet. As you go to open the door, calmly give the *wait* command. If he should attempt to push through the door, gently close it again, without saying anything and, of course, ensuring that you don't shut any part of him in the door! Each time you go to open the door, repeat the command **wait**.

Each time he attempts to push through, close the door again. Eventually, you will find that you can open the door further and further each time, until the dog waits whilst the door is opened fully. Place your hand on the dog's collar, praise him for waiting and give him a titbit. Take hold of his lead and call him forward, out of the car, using the same calling command that you will have taught him for coming when called.

You can further enforce the *wait* command at feeding times. After you have called him for his food, and rewarded him for coming with a small handful of his food, you can tell him to **sit** and **wait**. Place the food bowl on the floor (or feeding stand), and repeat the *wait* command. If he attempts to move, quietly pick the food up again. Then repeat the procedure, until the dog does not attempt to move, at which time you can give him an appropriate command, such as, 'OK' or 'That'll do', and allow him to have the food. The dog will quickly learn that after the *wait* command has been given he is

Fig. 17. As you go to the door, calmly give the *wait* command.

expected to remain where he is temporarily, until he is told to come forward.

Finally, some people teach the *stay* to cover all these things, plus staying in one place, but I firmly believe this confuses the dog, giving him one command to mean two different things and expecting him to know which one you mean. It also encourages him to break the *stay* command, as he will be continually on edge, waiting for further instructions. If you have taught him that **stay** means he *never* moves until you return to his side, there can be no doubt in his mind whatsoever. With the *wait*, you are teaching him that he is to wait until given further instruction.

Stand
Verbal Command – Dog's name and **stand**.

I'm sure that some readers are wondering why on earth they should teach their dog to stand on command and what practical purpose it would serve. Well, how about when you brush your dog? What about when he comes back from a muddy walk and you have to dry him? Think about when you have to take the dog to the vet – it's much easier for the vet to examine him if he's standing nice and still. I'm sure you can think of other occasions within your own lives when it would be very convenient if he stood still on command.

The *stand* is the gentlest of all exercises to teach and also one of the easiest. The verbal command **stand** is given very gently, unlike all other commands you have been using and is delivered in a 'sing-song' type of voice. It must sound completely different from the authoritative commands of **sit** and **down**. The aim is to teach him that on receiving the verbal and visual commands, he will stand up, keeping his front feet still and moving his back feet *backwards*.

Start with your dog sitting on your left, close to your leg. He doesn't need to be on a lead. Have a titbit in your right hand, holding it between your thumb and first two fingers. Position your hand so that it is *almost* touching the dog's nose, and then slowly move your hand straight out a couple of inches in front of his nose. (Fig. 18.)

He will want to follow the food, and will stretch out, probably attempting to stand as he does so. Don't say **stand** at this stage, as you again want him to work out what movement is required, as you did when teaching the *sit* and *down*. If he doesn't quite get up, place your left hand, between you and him, and gently tickle and lift under his tummy, in an upwards and *slightly* backwards direction. (Fig. 19.)

As soon as he is standing, give him the food, telling him, 'Good **stand**, clever dog', several times, and keep him standing still by continuing to tickle his tummy with your left hand, whilst your right hand gently tickles

Fig. 18. *Stand* – dog sitting on left, hand holding titbit being extended outward.

Fig. 19. *Stand* – dog starting to follow hand, being gently helped by tummy lift.

the front of his chest. (Fig. 20.)

He will probably be more than willing to stand there forever, as he is receiving such lovely inducement to do so! Eventually, you will want him to stand just on the verbal command, perhaps with the hand signal also, which you are teaching with the help of the titbit, but practise several times using all the inducements, until he really latches on to the idea. Make sure you keep your voice command light and very pleasant sounding. If you make it too commanding, or gruff, he will get confused and perhaps interpret it the wrong way, perhaps either lying down, or maybe not moving at all, as he is unclear just *what* is expected of him.

You may feel that it would be easier and more comfortable for you if you place your left arm *over* the dog to lift and tickle him into the position. What tends to happen if you do that is that the dog will lean against the arm that is doing the tickling, resulting in him

131

Fig. 20. *Stand* – dog standing on left, right hand tickling chest.

leaning away from you, and you having to shuffle sideways towards your dog, to keep him with you.

You may find that once he has stood up, he continues to move forwards. That is because you have continued to move your right hand, with the titbit, away from his nose. As soon as he has stood, keep your hand still, and he will have no reason to walk away from it – he wants the titbit which your hand is holding. Make sure that you don't move your hand either up or down, but keep it straight out in front of the dog when you are encouraging him to stand. Any movement in either direction could again lead to the dog being confused and interpreting the movement as either a *sit* or a *down* signal, as he has already learned those hand movements when you taught him those positions.

Finally, you may find it easier if you kneel down beside your dog to begin with when teaching this exercise – it is certainly easier if you have a small dog, but with a dog of any size, it will save you bending over and, being nearer to your dog, will make delivery of the hand signal, plus the lifting and tickling, much more definite.

Coming When Called – The Recall
Verbal Command – Dog's name followed by **come**.
Visual Signal – Arms outstretched, either side of your body.

Teaching a dog to come back when you want him is one of those things that is so easy to get wrong! The problem usually occurs when you expect the dog to return whilst out on exercise, where he's having fun and freedom, before you have shown him indoors *what* is expected when you call him. If he doesn't come to you indoors, each and every time you call him, you can be sure that when he is outside, with all the interesting smells and distractions that are present, he certainly will not want to give up his liberty in a hurry!

You may also have made the problem worse by acting illogically (as far as the dog is concerned) when he does eventually decide to come back, after you have been calling him for ages. It may be that you are late for an appointment, or it is pouring with rain (or both!), and you have been standing in the park, calling and calling, whilst your dog is either playing with another dog, or investigating the bushes. Finally he comes back. You are now very cross, so of course you are not very happy with him. On goes the lead, and off you march. You know, of course, that the dog understands that you are cross, and his freedom has been ended, because he was slow in coming back! *Oh no he doesn't!* What he learns from your behaviour is that coming back to you is very unrewarding, as you are so cross when he does return to you. And not only that, his liberty is taken away! Staying away from you is therefore much more fun and rewarding, as he keeps his freedom and can do what he wants.

Another easily developed habit is only calling the dog back when it is time to go home. The dog then very quickly learns that being called signifies the end of his freedom, so he is therefore reluctant to come back.

133

Getting it Right

Probably the most important underlying factor is the dog's expectancy when he hears his name being used. Does he only hear his name when something is being offered, or does he hear his name several times a day when he is not expected to respond? Usually, when the dog first arrives in the house, his name is used frequently during interaction with him, so that you can teach him his name. What then tends to happen is you, and the rest of the family, start using his name conversationally, when you are not expecting him to respond, i.e. you talk about the dog to one another, perhaps telling them what the dog has been up to whilst they were out of the house. Had you been observing the dog when you first started talking about him, rather than to him, you would have noticed that when he first heard his name being used, he would probably have looked up from whatever he was doing. Then, because no clear indication was given to him to elicit a response, he would have looked away and continued with what he was doing. That is how the rot sets in! He learns to ignore his name.

Because it is human nature to want to talk *about* the dog without always wanting the dog to come to us, the easiest way around this is slightly to adapt the dog's name when you want him to come to you, and *only* use that adaptation when you are calling the dog. Coupled with the dog receiving a worthwhile reward for responding, you will condition the dog always to return when he hears the slightly varied sound, whilst you can still talk about him to one another, using the original name. As an example, let's assume you have called your dog 'Ben'. You could adapt that to 'Bennyboy' when you want him to come to you. The name 'Molly' could be adapted to 'Mollypups', 'Sacha' could be 'Sachapash', 'Cassie' could be 'Cass-Cass', and so on. One of my own favourites I used with one of my dogs, who was named 'Otto' – he became 'Spottyboy', only don't expect me to explain how that was arrived at!

Once you've selected a new calling name, then you need to show the dog what is expected when that sound is used – this is where the food comes in again, firstly with the dog's daily meals, and then with titbits.

Dogs very quickly learn their mealtime routines – they know when it is time to be fed! Before you start preparing his meal, make sure that he is out of the room, possibly being held by someone else, but ensure that he has clear access through to you. Get the food ready, then, holding it just in front of you, at waist height, call the dog with his new calling name. He will have already heard the food being prepared and he will have certainly smelt it, so as he is released from being held, once you have called him, he will probably arrive at ninety miles an hour in front of you! Reward him verbally and give him his food immediately. Repeat this same procedure before every mealtime for at least a week.

Please don't make the dog sit when he reaches you. You want him to learn that he is being rewarded with his food for coming when called and NOT for sitting. Dog logic works on a 'last behaviour offered is what the reward is for' basis. If, when he reaches you after being called, you then tell him to sit, then feed him, the dog will associate the reward of his food for sitting, rather than coming when called.

After a couple of days of the mealtime rewarding, you can start with titbit training for recalls too. Start when the dog is literally next to you, say lying beside you when you're watching TV. Have the titbits handy and, when he is not looking at you, use his new recall name once, in a pleasant tone. When he looks up at you, or sits up to get even closer, reward him with a titbit, plus a verbal reward and a cuddle. You need to back up the titbit rewards with verbal and physical praise each time you use them, as eventually you will be dispensing with them most of the time. The dog needs to understand that rewards are not only of the edible variety!

Slowly build up the distance when you are recalling

indoors, during that first week. Start with the dog a couple of feet away, then five, then ten feet and so on. Only instant response from the dog gets rewarded. If you have to call more than twice, do not give him the titbit when he does get to you. He has to understand that the second he hears his name, he must return to you for the food, otherwise he doesn't get it.

During all this preparation time, you must not let the dog roam free whilst on exercise – you don't want to undo the training which you are doing indoors by putting it to the test before you are ready.

After that first week, you will then be ready to try the dog outside. There is one more part of the plot to follow though! For the past seven days, you have been conditioning the dog to return to you, on hearing his recall name, and in return being rewarded with either his meal or titbits. Once he is running free outside, there will be more distractions, which may encourage the dog to delay coming immediately, so you will need a slight edge! You're going to make sure that he will come back, by taking him out hungry!

Assuming the dog is fed twice a day, morning and evening, on the day BEFORE you are going to test out the recall whilst the dog is running free, *don't feed him the evening meal!* Make sure that he has access to water, as he can tolerate being deprived of food for a short while, but he *must* have water. You may feel very guilty, as the dog will probably start reminding you that dinner is due, but don't weaken. Think of the years ahead with a dog who is a pleasure to take out off the lead. Don't give him any titbits either. Be determined. Next day, *don't feed him his morning meal either*. Instead, prepare his morning meal in at least ten individual portions, in plastic bags. It may be a bit messy, but again, remember your long term aim and don't be put off. You've now got a very hungry dog on your hands. Take him out, with the plastic bags of food in your pockets. When you get to your usual walking place, let him off the lead and, as he starts to go away from you, IMMEDIATELY call him back, take hold of his collar and give him one of the portions of food, plus a huge cuddle. Always hold the collar first before releasing the food to the dog. If you don't, he may well end up snatching the food from your hand and running off again. Holding him also gives you the opportunity to be 'in charge', by giving him his freedom again – after a few seconds, give the dog permission to 'go play' and let him go. Leave him a couple of minutes, then repeat the procedure again. Do this throughout the walk, saving one last portion for when the walk is over and you need to re-attach him to his lead. You should now have a dog who has earned his breakfast, by coming back to you each time he was called (with his new recall name).

He can have his evening meal as usual, but all his breakfasts for at least the next week should be 'earned' whilst out walking. That should be long enough to have built up the conditioning in the dog's mind that being called means he gets fed *and* cuddled. After that first week, you can resume feeding normally at home, but save all the titbits for when you are out walking, making him earn them by coming when called.

Keep up with the praise and cuddles when he returns to you, and always use a happy sounding voice when you call him – don't ever take him for granted and NEVER lose your temper. Either of those reactions from you will result in the dog refusing to return to you, and finding other, more interesting and rewarding things to do.

Possible Problems
If your dog has previously learned that when he is off the lead he can ignore you, even if he comes every time you call him indoors, don't fall into the trap of chasing him, or trying to grab him. He will be much quicker than you can be, and, from the dog's perception, it becomes a game which he always wins. *NEVER* tell him off once he does deign to return to you. From your viewpoint, you are telling the dog off for not returning

immediately, and making you wait, possibly being late for work, or an appointment (they always seem to know when you're in a hurry, don't they!). From the dog's perception, he has finally decided to give up playing with another dog, or chasing rabbits, or digging a hole, etc., and when he gets back to you, you're cross! Rather than being pleased to see him, you tell him off, maybe, heaven forbid, you smack him! What does he learn? Returning to you is UNPLEASANT. Staying away from you is far more rewarding.

There are some things you can do in that situation. STOP calling him – he's ignoring you anyway. If safe to do so, walk away from the dog. (Obviously if he's close to a road, that is not a good idea.) Sit on the grass and pretend to be ever so interested in something on the ground right in front of you. Dogs are curious creatures, and he may well come back to see what you are finding so fascinating. When he does return. DON'T GRAB HIM. Greet him warmly, and offer him a titbit, at the same time gently placing your hand on his collar. Reward him profusely, give him another titbit and then *let him go again*. If you don't, he definitely won't come back the next time you let him off his lead.

If a dog has had an unpleasant experience in the past connected with coming when called, or because of poor training has learnt not to come back, you may need to resort to putting him on a long line – about fifty feet – and letting him trail that behind him, so that you can either take hold, or stand on it, to prevent the dog from running off. It is not ideal though, and often once you let them off the line, they immediately return to their old habits. You may ultimately have to opt for a compromise, and keep your dog on an extending lead – that way at least the dog can run a short way and have some freedom of movement.

When the walk is over, don't always call him at the same spot in the park. He will quickly learn the route of his walk, and will start to associate 'that spot' with the end of his freedom, and may well start to run off or ignore you when you get to the usual place.

Retrieving

Most dogs will quite naturally want to chase after
articles thrown for them. The difficult part is getting
them to return the articles, so that they can be thrown
again! Of course, you should not start with retrieving
until you have taught the dog to come back to you!

One word of caution here – if you want the dog to
fetch a ball, please make sure that the ball is bigger than
the dog's throat. As an example, a tennis ball could
easily get lodged in the throat of a Labrador or German
Shepherd Dog. At the risk of being a killjoy, even
throwing sticks can be dangerous – if the stick does not
land flat, but 'javelins' into the ground, the dog could
impale himself on it. There are many purpose-designed
toys available from your pet shop which are safe for the
dog to chase and bring back to you.

If you want your dog to play 'fetch', then you have to
be very careful about chastising the dog if he should run
off with an inappropriate article indoors – if he should
'steal' a shoe, for example, and you shout and run after
him, all he learns is that the shoe must be very important, as you are trying so hard to take it away from him.
This actually encourages him to hang onto it. The shoe
becomes prey in the mind of the dog, and basic instincts
will come to the fore – he may even show signs of
aggression if you try and take it away from him. After
that, he will most certainly not want to bring back a
play article in the park. Whilst you don't want to
encourage the dog to steal things, what you should do
when he has an inappropriate article in his mouth is to
encourage him to bring it to you, and reward him with a
titbit when he does. This will not stop him taking things,
but it will stop him running off with them! It may also
help enforce the rule which all members of the family
should adhere to – don't leave things around that you
wouldn't want the dog to pick up!

If you start off indoors, rewarding him with a titbit

when he brings his toys to you, that behaviour will be repeated when you throw a toy for him outside.

Perhaps at some stage you may want to do more formal obedience with your dog, with a view to entering obedience competitions. A formal retrieve will be much easier to teach if you have started off as described above, having already conditioned the dog that bringing the retrieve article back is a good thing, as he gets rewarded for doing so.

Walking on the Lead
Verbal Command – Dog's name (for attention) and initially **steady**. When **steady** has been taught, choose either **heel** or **close**.

A dog who pulls continually is not a pleasure to take out. You may be lucky in getting one of those rare animals who doesn't try and pull, but most dogs will try and 'take the lead', usually because they want to take control as leader of the 'hunt', as that is how a dog perceives going for a walk with his owner.

Pulling on the lead is second only to recall problems as the exercise that owners seem to have the most trouble with, and I suspect that some of you may have turned straight to these pages, without reading the preceding ones! If you *have* done that, please read the previous pages first, as everything written so far has been designed to help with overall control, culminating in making this exercise easier to teach.

Two of the many reasons why a dog pulls is that being on the lead is boring and restricting. Boring because he cannot keep stopping to investigate and sniff, and restricting because you are trying to make him walk where *you* want, i.e. at your side, rather than where *he* wants to be, i.e. out in front. It tends to become one long battle, with you pulling each other, and each attempt by you to pull him back makes him more determined to pull forward. Sometimes it becomes such an ordeal for owners that they stop trying, either by not putting the dog on the lead at all (extremely foolish and dangerous, not to say against the law if on a road), or by tolerating the dog pulling and keeping the lead walks to a minimum, and ending up with a sore shoulder and arm in the process. Have I struck a chord yet?

So, how can you make walking on the lead a happier process for you both and at the same time teach the dog not to pull? You can't expect the dog to walk forward without pulling if he cannot stand still on the lead without pulling, so that is your starting point. However, before you begin, a word of caution. The flick type action that I mention later is designed simply to off-balance the dog. *It is not meant to choke him or cause him pain.* It will have the effect of momentarily stopping him. Please don't be heavy handed by jerking, pulling or tugging the lead. Finally, only flick the lead if you have an adult dog. DO NOT PUT ANY PRESSURE ON A PUPPY'S NECK, just use the verbal command, followed by the praise and the titbit.

What you want to aim for is the dog walking nicely on

Fig. 21. Walking correctly.

a loose lead, not 'glued' to your leg, but without continually trying to take up the slack. He is allowed to walk slightly in front of you, provided he is not pulling. (Fig. 21.) Walking to heel, really close to your leg, is not what we're aiming at here – that can come later. You can also teach this without putting any special collar around the dog's neck – again, for more precise work, you may do well to purchase a double action check collar – NOT A CHOKE CHAIN – but for now, a normal, flat, leather collar will suffice, together with a leather or nylon lead, about three or four feet long. (Fig. 22.)

Don't try teaching the dog not to pull when you're on the way out for the first walk of the day. The dog will be so excited at going out that you will have a hard task on your hands just to get him to pay attention, let alone not to pull. The best place to begin teaching the dog is in the garden. Attach the lead to the dog's collar and *stand still*. Make up your mind now which side the dog is going to walk on – left or right – and stick to it. You don't want the dog to be continually swapping sides in front of you. Hold the lead with both hands close together, at the end of the lead. Have a few titbits in one hand. If the dog makes no attempt to pull, tell him, 'Good **steady**', and give him a titbit. All the time he

Fig. 22. A normal, flat, leather collar, together with a leather or nylon lead, will suffice.

makes no attempt to pull, keep verbally rewarding him. *Keep standing still*. When he makes the first effort to pull and take up the slack of the lead, give a *little gentle* flick on the lead, so that it momentarily tightens, and then release the tension so that the lead goes slack again. *Keep standing still*. As you flick the lead, give the command **steady**. The flick will have the effect of slightly unbalancing the dog, which will make him turn and look at you, having the effect of slackening the lead. Reward the dog for both looking at you and taking the pressure off.

Repeat the flick of the lead each time the dog attempts to take up the slack, and reward him each time he responds to the flick and **steady** word. Make sure that there is obvious slack in the lead between each flick. Don't rush the procedure, and don't be tempted to walk yet – keep still. Don't worry if the dog decides to sit – just take a couple of steps backwards to get him up on his feet.

When the dog is happy to stand, with the lead slack, for about ten seconds (count it out under your breath), take one step forward. If the dog tries to pull again, stand still immediately and flick the lead again, using the **steady** command. Make it clear to the dog that, if he pulls, you stand still, and after each attempt and correction, ensure the dog realises what has happened before you attempt another step forward.

For this first lesson, you want to aim for about ten paces without the dog pulling. Walk at a speed which is comfortable for you and don't allow the dog to dictate how fast you go. All the time the dog is walking without taking up the slack of the lead, tell him what a clever dog he is. The time involved on this first lesson varies from dog to dog, but shouldn't last longer than about fifteen minutes. When you have achieved the first objective of ten paces without pulling, give the dog a big fuss and let him off the lead for a romp. Don't overdo the practice sessions – short regular lessons are far more beneficial than one or two long ones. Puppies especially, have a relatively short attention span, and you will only bore the puppy by training for more than ten minutes at a time, for a maximum of three times a day. Leave at least a couple of hours between each session.

Over a few sessions of regular practice, provided you are completely consistent, don't lose your temper, reward the dog lavishly all the time he is getting it right and keep the training sessions fun, you will have a dog who, whilst not walking 'to heel', will be walking nicely without pulling, making the whole process much more enjoyable for both of you!

Having achieved at least several steps without pulling, now you want to show him that sometimes he has to walk closer to you, rather than at the end of the lead. For this, you will need lots of inducement in the shape of titbits or, if your dog likes to play with toys, his favourite toy. Decide which command you are going to use, either **heel** (pronounced HEYALL) or **close** (pronounced CLOWSS). Position him sitting on your left, with his right shoulder close to and almost touching your left leg (Fig. 23.) That is the ideal heel position, which you want him to keep to when he is walking. Hold the lead in your right hand, with the titbit or toy in your left hand. Place the 'inducement' an inch or so in front of his nose, and step off on your *left* foot, using the command **heel** or **close**. You step off left foot first as an added signal that he is to be with you – remember when teaching the *sit and down stay*, you always moved right foot first, as he had to remain behind.

After taking two paces, give him the inducement, take a step back and PLAY with him, either interacting with him and the toy, or, if you're not using a toy, have a play just with him. After half a minute or so, set him up again and repeat the two paces. When he is nice and steady doing two paces, do four, then six and so on, building up slowly, over several sessions, until he will walk for twenty or thirty paces beside your left leg, keeping his shoulder level with your leg and not pulling.

All the time he is walking nicely, verbally reward him,

Fig. 23. Prior to starting heelwork.

tickle him gently on the top of his head, or on his right ear. (Fig. 24.) Tell him how wonderful he is, and, without stopping walking, give him a titbit every three or four paces. Tell him, whilst you are walking, what a good heel (or close) he is doing. Remember that you want him to associate the verbal command with his action of walking nicely, so keep repeating it. If you're using a toy, let him have the toy to hold a couple of times during the session, again without stopping walking.

Keep the sessions short – no more than ten minutes at the most, two or three times a day. Over about a week, you will have conditioned him to walk properly at heel. You will have taught him that being on the lead is FUN, as he gets food, and/or a toy. He will be receiving

Fig. 24. *Heel* – dog walking nicely, getting rewarded.

constant, positive attention from you when he remains close to you. There will not be any discomfort for him to fight, as previously when you have had a 'tug of war' with him.

The other positive outcome of teaching him this way is that you will have developed two different modes of walking. One, with the *heel* or *close* command, means that he has to stay next to your left leg, as needed on a busy road, or when there are crowds of people about, and two, with the *steady* command, meaning that as long as he doesn't pull, he can be out at the end of the lead, in circumstances where he would not be causing a nuisance to anyone or be in danger.

Possible Problems
If the dog is still trying to pull, it may be that you are causing him to do so, by 'hanging' on to the lead too

tightly (see Fig. 25). You must give him a chance to walk nicely by starting with a loose lead, and immediately you have given him the steady signal, ensure that the lead is loose again. As he attempts to take up the slack of the lead, gently flick the lead to signal the collar and take a small step to your right simultaneously. This will have the effect of increasing the off-balancing action of the signal.

Perhaps you are holding the lead with your left hand as well as your right (Fig. 26), trying to stop the dog getting in front of you to start with. This is counter-productive, not only because it ties up your left hand, which you need to be free to give the praise and titbits, but also because it tends to make you pull the lead back with your left hand. Also, even if you are still attempting to give the flick signal with your right hand, the first

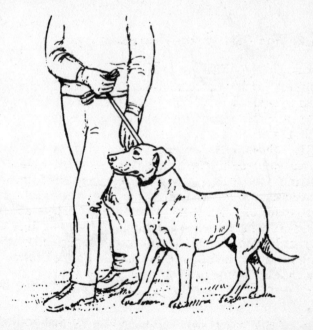

Fig. 25. *Heel* – lead too short.

object that signal will connect with is your left hand, not the dog!

You may be trying to walk too quickly, so that the dog is trying to race you. The quicker your dog wants to walk, the *slower* you should walk. He is being taught to walk at your pace, not the other way around!

LAGGING

Maybe your dog is nervous when on the lead, perhaps lagging behind you. If that is the case, *do not put any pressure on the collar*. Turn to face him whilst still walking, continue to walk backwards in the same direction, slow your pace and use *loads* of encouragement, clap your hands, offer titbits and cuddles and use a

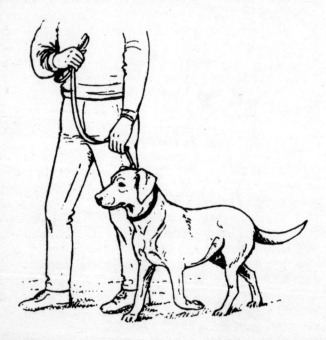

Fig. 26. *Heel* – lead held incorrectly, left hand holding half way up.

reassuring, confident voice. If you try to 'baby' him, he will simply become even more nervous. Adopt the attitude of 'Everything's fine, I'm in charge, so nothing nasty is going to happen'. A sort of jolly hockey sticks approach! To make walking on the lead even nicer for him, always put him on the lead before every nice event in his life, i.e. every meal time, and when people he knows come to call. Make the lead the prelude to nice things happening.

GETTING THE DOG TO RETURN TO HEEL FROM ANY POSITION

There will be times when your dog manages to position himself in the wrong place, just as you want to start walking with him. You have probably been 'scooping' him back to your left side with your hands, which will only have made him want to sit incorrectly even more. He likes being touched and so repeats the action which makes you touch him!

Using the commands which, by now, will be meaning **heel** to the dog, you are going to show him how to get there on his own, without your having to touch him. Obviously you will use exactly the same signals as you have been using to teach him to be by your left leg, as this is where you want him to be.

To show him how to move into the correct position, he must first of all be in the wrong one. For the purpose of teaching, start with him sitting in front of you – something which happens very easily if you are too slow with the *sit* command when you come to a halt.

To set this up, incorporate the *wait* command which you have already taught him. Start with him sitting by your left leg, command him to **wait** and step around to face him, close to his front feet, as in Fig. 27. Now you are going to stand still and he is going to move around behind you, going past your right leg and ending up on your left-hand side.

Gather the slack of the lead up in your right hand, without putting any pressure on the collar, and give him

Fig. 27. Ready to return to the *heel* position from the front.

the command which you have already taught him to mean 'be by my left leg'. Have a titbit hidden in your *right* hand. At this stage he will probably look confused, as he won't be able to work out *how* to get to your left leg, even though he knows that is where you want him. Pat your left leg with your left hand, and guide the dog towards your right leg, showing him the titbit. As soon as his head is level with your right leg, reach around behind you with your left hand and take hold of the lead and the titbit, at the same time looking over your left shoulder as far as you can, until you can catch your dog's eye. (See Fig. 28.)

Continue to encourage him round, with your voice

150

Fig. 28. Dog being guided around handler, following hand holding titbit.

and the titbit, and as his head appears beside your left leg, change the lead and titbit back into your right hand and, as his shoulder gets level with your left leg, tell him to sit and give him the titbit and lots of praise. (See Fig. 29.)

Now, all that is a great deal more complicated to write down than actually do! Follow the pictures carefully and you will see it is quite simple really. It helps if your dog can see your face as he is coming around behind you. Once he is up and moving, turn your head around to your left, so that you can see him coming and greet him as he comes around. Remember to keep your feet still. You must remain stationary; he is moving to you, not you to him.

If you are having trouble getting the initial movement from your dog (i.e. getting him up from the sit position),

151

Fig. 29. Dog completing the exercise, being given titbit.

you can, just to start with, take a step back with your right foot as you give him the first heel signal. This gives you a little more 'impetus'. As soon as he is up and moving, you must put your right foot level with the left one. Don't leave it out behind you, or your dog will have to walk out and around you to get to the heel position, making him go very wide and giving you more trouble in controlling him.

When you've practised this exercise a few times and your dog understands what you want, start getting him to come to heel from any direction. Again using the *wait* command, start with him sitting by your left leg, tell him **wait** and step forward one pace, stand still and call him up to heel, using full commands and signals. Again, with him sitting by your left leg, take a step sideways, away from him, then call him to **heel**, this time continuing to walk forwards as he comes to you.

152

If you are determined and patient, and don't try to take any shortcuts, your dog will soon accept being on the lead, without trying to pull. Be consistent, reward him at every opportunity and remember to try and make it fun and interesting. Have little chats with him whilst you are walking, to keep his attention on you. Passers-by will think you are a little mad, but if it helps to make heelwork more of a pleasure for you both, does it really matter what strangers think of you?

Head Collars
If you still find you are having difficulty getting the dog to walk nicely, you could try one of the head collars which are now available for dogs. They have the effect of encouraging the dog not to pull, by restraining the dog's head. They do take some getting used to though, and not all dogs will accept them. If you elect to try one, take the dog to the pet shop with you when you go, so that, firstly, you get the right size and, secondly, so that you can be shown how to fit the head collar and how it works.

Fig. 30. Head collars encourage the dog not to pull by restraining the dog's head.

More Advanced Training
Once you have completed the basic training, and if you and your dog have enjoyed learning together, you may want to continue your dog's education, perhaps with the ultimate goal of competing in the various forms of obedience that have become popular. Any dog can be taught more advanced obedience, and even though breeds such as Border Collies, German Shepherd Dogs, Labradors and Retrievers tend to proliferate, there is no reason why your crossbreed or Terrier could not do well in competition.

Obedience Competitions
You should find a training club with instructors who specialise in motivational training techniques and who can advise you on the finer points required in the ring. Your dog should be energetic and willing to play with you to achieve the best results, and you will also need to be enthusiastic and determined. To train a dog to the high standard required demands a regular commitment of time and effort and a self-disciplined approach to your technique. The best way to find out if this is the sport for you is to attend some shows as a spectator and talk to experienced competitors – most are happy to help but try not to approach them as they are about to enter the ring!

Shows take place all over the country at various levels – Exemption, Limited, Open and Championship. Exemption shows are often held in conjunction with other events such as fetes and may have one or two classes suitable for those new to the sport. At this level your dog does not need to be registered with the Kennel Club. If you wish to compete at Limited, Open or Championship shows, registration with the Kennel Club is compulsory. If you have a crossbreed or Mongrel, or an unregistered Border Collie, you will need to apply to the Obedience and Working Trials Register at the Kennel Club. If you have a pedigree dog, you should already have the registration certificate from the breeder and have had the ownership transferred to your name (see page 51). If you wish to enter a show before you have received your registration or transfer certificate you must add NAF (Name Applied For) or TAF (Transfer Applied For) after your dog's name on the entry form.

Exemption shows are often advertised in the local press. There is a publication called *Dog Training Weekly* which gives details of forthcoming shows, plus show reports, and also contains some interesting training articles. *DTW* is only available by postal subscription – see page 251 for details.

At all Kennel Club registered shows there are up to five classes covering different levels. Pre-Beginners is the lowest class and involves Heel work, both on and off the lead, a Recall and a Sit and Down Stay. The other classes are Beginners, Novice, Class A, Class B and Class C. Exercises in the higher classes include Scent Discrimination and Distant Control, as well as more advanced heel work and retrieving.

By winning three of the highest classes – Championship C – under three different judges, a dog can gain the title of Obedience Champion. For dogs who have won their way through the classes there is also the award known as the Obedience Warrant, signified by the letters OW after the dog's name. Each year at Crufts, all dogs and bitches that have won a Championship C in the previous year are invited to take part in the Kennel Club Obedience Championships. At this level competition is at an extremely high standard, with even minor faults resulting in loss of points.

Competitive obedience can be a very rewarding hobby, with the opportunity to make new friends and have fun with your dog. It is relatively inexpensive and requires no complicated equipment. You don't need an expensive dog either – many people compete successfully with rescued dogs. For the younger competitor there are also special classes arranged by the Kennel Club Junior Organisation, and for all well-trained pet dogs there is the Kennel Club Good Citizen Scheme, which is a test rather that a competition.

Working Trials

Working Trials predate Obedience Competitions and have their roots in service dog training. They were designed as a practical test of working ability and cover a wide range of activities including nose work and agility.

There are five different stakes – Companion Dog (CD), Utility Dog (UD), Working Dog (WD), Tracking Dog (TD) and Patrol Dog (PD). Dogs which achieve a qualifying mark in each group of exercises within a class at a Championship Trial are entitled to have the letters CD, UD, WD, TD or PD after their names. In addition, winners of TD or PD classes at Championship Trials are awarded Working Trial Certificates, which count towards the title of Working Trials Champion. The CD and UD stakes have jumps that relate to the height of the dog and there is consequently more variety in the breeds that are entered. The higher stakes have full height jumps and the most common breeds entered are German Shepherds and Border Collies/Working Sheepdogs, with some Labradors, Retrievers and a few other larger working breeds.

As Working Trials include nose work exercises such as searching and tracking, they are usually held on private land and therefore are not so accessible to spectators as some other canine sports. To get started in trials, you will need a good standard of obedience, a fit dog with sound hips and a love of the outdoors! The Kennel Club can provide a list of Working Trial Societies that will be able to help with further information and advice. Working Trials is a more specialist sport than Competitive Obedience and you may have to travel longer distances for tuition and competitions.

Agility

Agility competitions are one of the more recent sports to develop, but have quickly gained a following with competitors and spectators. It is extremely rewarding for the dogs, as it gives them something really interesting to do and, like obedience competitions, keeps the dog's brain active in a positive way. Like the other sports, Kennel Club registration is a must, and dogs must be 18 months or over to compete in agility. The main reason for this is that the dog's bones may be damaged by jumping at an early age and it is recommended that training does not start until the dog is at least one year old – later still with the larger breeds.

You will need to be physically fit, as you have to run around the ring with the dog as he goes over or through each obstacle. Obstacles range from a variety of different jumps, rather like those used in show jumping, to more specialised equipment such as weaving poles, tunnels and walkways. Accuracy is an important feature – not only must the dog jump cleanly and follow the correct course to avoid penalty points, but on some obstacles the dog must touch marked contact points. In addition, time penalties may be added to the total score if the dog fails to meet the set time for the course. A clear round is therefore quite an achievement and is often rewarded with a special rosette.

Agility competitions have become very popular and attract large entries. The standard is very high and there is sometimes very little difference in marks between the placings. There are various classes, including some for smaller dogs – known as mini-agility – and it is great fun to see these little dogs racing around the course at top speed. Dogs taking part in agility do enjoy themselves and can get over-excited so it is important that basic obedience control is attained before tackling agility.

Agility training often takes place at indoor riding schools where the facilities are suitable for jumping, and there are classes held all over the country. As with the other sports, the Kennel Club can provide details of clubs registered with them.

Showing
Unlike obedience, agility or working trials, showing classes are judged on the look and conformation of

your dog, and on how he or she matches up to the breed standard, as laid down by the Kennel Club. It helps if you mention to the breeder, when buying, that you would like to show your puppy, so that you purchase a good-quality puppy initially.

As well as being obedient in the show ring, you will need to know how to show your particular breed, so attending a Ringcraft Training Club is very helpful. You will encounter some of the atmosphere and distractions that your puppy will have to cope with at shows, and at the same time will also receive advice on standing and handling your puppy from knowledgeable enthusiasts. Joining fees are not high, and most good clubs run regular match nights, which provide good experience for you and your puppy, emulating where possible what will happen in the show ring. Your puppy must be at least six months old before you can enter him in a show, and must be registered with the Kennel Club, with the exception of Exemption shows (see page 154), which are a really good place to start your showing career. You can enter these types of show on the actual show day. The other types of shows are as follows:

1.   Limited Shows – These are limited to members of the club which is running them, so you have to join that particular club in order to compete. The membership fee is usually small, and you can usually join the club when you receive your entry form. These shows are advertised in the dog press, and entry is always in advance – you cannot enter on the day of the show.

2.   Open Shows – These are held throughout the country and will have individual classes for most breeds. If your particular breed does not have an individual class, you can enter in what is called Any Variety – where you will be competing against different breeds. You do not need to be a member of the organising club to compete at these shows. Again, they are advertised in the dog press, and you must enter your dog in advance of the actual show.

3. Championship Shows – These are where you will meet stiff competition, with classes being quite large. Entry into a Championship show is the same as that for Open shows. A dog can only become a show champion by competing and winning at a Championship show. The classes for your breed will be split into separate classes for dogs and bitches. When all classes for dogs (males) have been judged, all class winners then compete against each other for the title of Best Dog, and this dog will be awarded a Challenge Certificate. The Reserve dog (2nd) will be awarded the Reserve Challenge Certificate. The bitches are then judged, for Best Bitch and Reserve Bitch, and again they will receive a Challenge Certificate and Reserve Challenge Certificate. The Best Dog and Best Bitch then compete against each other for the title of Best of Breed. The winner will then go forward into what is called the Group judging, where all other winning dogs from breeds in the same group definition compete for the title Best of Group. When all Group winners are decided, they then compete against each other for the title Best in Show. A dog or bitch must win three separate challenge certificates, under three different judges, to become a champion. The last of the three certificates must be won when the dog is over one year old.

4. Crufts – Dogs who win at Championship Shows, or who gain Best Puppy in Show, Best in Show and Reserve Best in Show at an all breeds open show, can qualify to compete at Crufts. Only a dog of nine months or over can compete – if a dog has qualified but will be too young to compete, he or she will be able to compete the following year without further qualification.

Showing your dog can be great fun, and you will meet other like-minded people and owners of the same breed as your dog. Do remember though, that your dog is first and foremost a pet, and not an ornament, and remember too, if you show your dog, that whatever the outcome you always go home with the best dog!

Information about all these types of training can often be obtained from your local library or veterinary surgery, or by contacting The Kennel Club (see Appendix, page 252).

10

The Aggressive Dog

Sadly, some dogs are, or become, aggressive. It is difficult to generalise over possible cures without seeing and assessing each individual case, but I will go into some of the causes and suggest ways to cope.

If you have a dog who likes to bite, be it other dogs, strangers, family members or even yourself, you may possibly have already thought about muzzling him, re-homing him, or even having him put to sleep.

A muzzle, or some other kind of head restraint, may well stop him from biting, but it won't teach him *not* to, nor help you to find out why he wants to bite in the first place. Re-homing him is simply passing on the problem to somebody else, which is hardly very fair to them or to the dog. The last resort, having the dog painlessly destroyed, should only be considered when you have explored every possible avenue available to you.

What makes a dog aggressive? It could be anything from bad treatment in a previous home, accidental mistreatment, or poor basic training, through to poor breeding, medical ailments or the diet he is being fed.

Bad Treatment in a Previous Home
If you have a 'rescued' dog, you may well not have been given the real reason why the dog needed a new home, either by a previous owner or the rescue kennels, even if they knew the true reason in the first place.

People who mistreat dogs fall into two groups – those who are deliberately cruel or those who are cruel through ignorance. The result, however, is the same: a dog who is confused, who will use aggression either to protect himself, or to get his own way.

Despite the bad treatment and subsequent confusion, the dog will still feel insecure when he leaves his 'family' and enters a new one. At first he may behave gratefully and, depending on the basic nature of the dog, this period may be very short, or last for ages. Provided that you are consistent in what you will allow him to do and what you will not permit, in a fair and logical way, the dog should settle in with his new family and will know where he stands. However, if his treatment in the previous home was not consistent, or indeed was deliberately cruel, at some stage he will try to test you, in an attempt to establish his position within the new pack.

If, in the past, he has used aggression as a form of self defence against unfair treatment, or to get what he wanted, he may try to continue to use that behaviour with you. Your reaction to any show of aggression from your dog should depend on the circumstances which initially provoked it.

It may be that the dog has learned to steal and guard a 'trophy', hiding under a table or chair. Here you should avoid a confrontational approach. DO NOT be tempted to drag him out – there lies the path to being bitten! Leave the dog alone, vacate the room, shutting the door behind you. Leave him for half an hour, then return, acting calmly and avoiding eye contact with him. He'll probably come to greet you, leaving his 'den' and his trophy. IGNORE the stolen item, make a fuss of the dog and leave the room again, this time letting him follow you – don't call him out, or he'll probably rush back to get the item. Give him a treat and, making sure he doesn't follow you, go back into the room and remove the offending item!

In future, try to prevent that situation happening. If he's stealing things and bolting to a place of safety, then ensure that there is nothing around to steal! If he's just using the 'bolt-holes' to avoid you, or avoid what he thinks is going to be punishment, remove access to these areas – block them up, move furniture, etc.

In milder cases, when the dog may just 'grumble' at you, say, for instance, he doesn't want to be brushed, or dried with a towel, a firm NO and a steady stare at the dog should be enough. He may well have been hurt in the past when being groomed, so it is hardly surprising that he should defend himself. Don't shout or scream at him – that will just make him grumble even more. Assuming he does stop, this is one case when you DON'T tell him he's a good dog – you only reward the dog when he does something good, not for NOT doing something naughty! When the grumbling stops, just speak calmly to the dog, then make him do something, i.e. sit or down, which you can then reward. This will also further support your role as pack leader – insisting that the dog perform some task for you, which you can then praise.

Once you have established the 'trigger' which provokes the dog, you can either ensure that these situations are avoided, or set up a controlled situation, in order to overcome them. It may be a particular noise, person, place or thing which triggers the defensive aggression.

As an example, let's use the case of a dog whose previous owner used to beat him. Suppose the owner also had a motor-bike and consequently wore a crash helmet. The dog therefore has a remembered association between people wearing crash helmets and pain. You may have owned the dog for some time, but during that time the dog has not come into contact with anyone wearing a helmet. Then one day an innocent visitor arrives at your house by motor-bike and enters your home, either wearing or carrying the helmet. Suddenly, your previously placid, friendly dog becomes a snarling, biting maniac. Exit one visitor, hopefully not hurt, but definitely unimpressed! Your next step is to borrow a crash helmet. Start to treat it as an extension of your-self, carrying it around with you, leaving it beside your chair when you sit down. Be very calm and casual about it, not making any direct reference to the helmet as far

163

as the dog is concerned. Once the dog is used to you walking around with the helmet, start wearing it for a few minutes, several times a day. When he accepts that, leave the helmet by the dog's bowl, until he accepts it completely and ignores it.

The next stage is to set up a dummy situation, of a visitor wearing the helmet and arriving at your house. Enlist the help of a member of the family, or a friend whom the dog knows and likes. Make sure the visitor has plenty of dog-type titbits in his pocket. Invite the visitor in, sit him down and talk calmly to him and the dog. Provided there has been no sign of aggression from the dog, the visitor is to offer the dog a titbit, talking to him very calmly and quietly. He must not make any sudden moves, or try to touch the dog at this stage.

Any mumbling or grumbling from the dog must be ignored. There must not be any unpleasant connection with the visitor as far as the dog is concerned, and if you told him off in this situation, the dog would associate the visitor with your displeasure, resulting in him being even more determined not to make friends. When all has been calm for about ten minutes, the visitor can start to stroke the dog, again offering more titbits.

Once the dog is totally at ease with the visitor, tell him to remove the helmet and place it on the floor beside him. Try putting a titbit inside the helmet, encouraging the dog to seek it out. Repeat this whole procedure two or three times over a couple of weeks, using different people each time.

What you are showing the dog is that the situation, i.e. a person wearing a helmet, is no longer a threatening one for him and nothing dreadful is going to happen. All the time he is good, he receives affection and reward, in the shape of stroking and titbits.

Eventually, people wearing crash helmets will only provoke pleasant associations for the dog – you may even end up with him actively seeking out people wearing helmets. However, that's another problem!

Apply this type of therapy to whatever is provoking

the dog into defensive aggressive behaviour. Although it may seem odd not to chastise the dog for showing aggression, in these situations being punished will simply cause the bad behaviour to escalate. Reward all acts of compliance profusely – remember, once again, that the dog will repeat actions that get your attention and learn quickly *not* to repeat actions that get ignored.

Accidental Mistreatment

This could range from you accidentally treading on your dog's foot, to touching the dog where he has an injury of which you were unaware. Such occasions will stick in your dog's mind as an experience which he will not want repeated.

Let's take the instance when you have accidentally trodden on your dog's foot. No doubt you were very sorry, and in spite of the fact that he snapped at you, you forgave him because it was your fault. You probably even gave him a cuddle, in an attempt to appease him. After that first occasion, he becomes more and more edgy whenever you, or indeed anyone, steps near his feet, and either starts flying out to attack, or alternatively running away from them, as he associates the proximity of the feet with the discomfort. How do you solve this without being confrontational and without resorting to punishment as a reinforcement to show your dislike of such behaviour?

You will need to set up a situation, whilst you are wearing boots on your legs for protection, and so stopping you from having any reaction to his aggression. You have to show him that he is not always going to be hurt when people step near him. You are also going to have to tolerate him snapping at you, until he realises that (a) he isn't going to be hurt and (b) snapping at you isn't going to stop you stepping near him. Have plenty of titbits ready. Have a long line attached to his collar, so that you can stop him running away from you, but do not be tempted to use the line as a form of correction. It is simply there to ensure the dog remains in close proximity.

So, with your feet and legs protected by the boots, start walking slowly towards the dog, a step at a time. As you take each step, speak to him soothingly and, provided the dog hasn't either tried to run or tried to bite, place a titbit on the floor by your foot. Stand still on one foot and gently swing your foot around, close to your dog's face. Again, reward for no reaction, ignore any aggressive reaction. Place a titbit on your foot, letting him take it in his own time. Stand still right in front of him and scatter titbits all around and on your feet. All the time, speak to him gently and lovingly, reinforcing his good behaviour with lots of 'good dog', etc.

Depending on the nature of your dog, and how much discomfort he experienced when you first accidentally trod on him, this desensitising may take only a couple of days, or a couple of weeks. I would suggest that you do it at least twice a day, for ten minutes each time. When he has accepted your feet being close to him without trying either to attack, or run from you, for at least a week, repeat the whole process wearing soft shoes, and end up actually 'stroking' your dog with your feet, liberally rewarding him with titbits and cuddles all the time he accepts the situation. Any sign of grumbling must be completely ignored, and all the time he is grumbling, stop the titbits and don't talk to him at all.

Eventually, with patience, you will overcome this problem. Like the helmet situation, if your dog develops a phobia about any normal situation, or a particular sound, apply the same type of therapy. Even if the situation appears ridiculous to you, be aware of the dog's feelings and act accordingly. To put the whole thing onto a human basis, it is much like someone getting cross with you if you are terrified of spiders. It doesn't matter how cross they get, or how stupid they think you are, you just can't tolerate spiders, and their anger, or derision, just makes the whole situation even more stressful. That is exactly how the dog feels!

Incorrect Basic Training

Dogs do not naturally know right from wrong. Unfortunately many owners unintentionally allow their dogs to become aggressive, by permitting certain behaviour. This is especially so with young puppies, when signs of aggression are allowed because 'he's only a baby'. It can also happen when you give a home to a rescued dog. You try to compensate him for the trauma he has gone through, by being too soft and feeling sorry for him.

In the same way, dogs who are not given the opportunity to socialise with other people and/or dogs, will often show aggressive tendencies when they do eventually come into contact with people and dogs they do not know.

It is obviously better for all concerned to socialise the dog properly. By socialise, I mean regular interaction with other people, dogs, other animals, places, etc. During these periods of socialising, the dog learns valuable lessons in the correct way to interact with people and dogs, from the reactions *he* receives in response to his behaviour. If he is of a nervous disposition, he will learn that if he runs from another dog, he will probably be chased, whilst if he stays still, no harm will come to him. If he is of a 'pushy' nature, he will most likely be put in his place if he should barge up to another dog.

Introduce the dog properly to the world outside his home. Then he will not feel threatened by other people or dogs. There is often a tendency for under-socialised dogs to be protective towards their owners. Most dogs, once they are secure with those they know well, will assume that strangers are equally trustworthy, unless those strangers show warning signs to the contrary.

Some people, either deliberately or through ignorance, may tease the dog into aggressive behaviour. Children, especially those who have not been taught to respect animals, often end up the victim of their own actions, when a dog retaliates against constant teasing.

Other people may be genuinely afraid of dogs, giving off confusing 'vibes' to the dog, which could cause him to act in an aggressively defensive manner.

You are responsible for your dog's actions, so you must be aware how his behaviour is perceived by others. Even if you know absolutely that he is not going to be aggressive, his behaviour may be sending out the wrong signals, or may be being misinterpreted. If the subject of either the real or perceived aggression has innocently sparked off the behaviour, explain to him or her (in a reasonable manner, of course!) what the action was that initiated the dog's behaviour.

Obviously you will not be rewarding your dog for any displays of aggression, but once the incident is resolved, immediately put the dog in the position of doing something for you, even something as simple as sitting, so that you can reward him for *that* behaviour, showing him which type of behaviour gets rewarded, i.e. being obedient. If he is on the lead at the time, do make sure that you don't put any pressure on the lead.

A tight lead can indicate to the dog that there is something to be on guard against. In the same way, tightening the lead in an attempt to stop him showing aggression in the first place will probably provoke him further, into an aggressive display. It can also make the dog feel safe, as by hanging on to him, you are effectively keeping him out of trouble. The dog then feels that you are protecting him, which encourages aggressive displays, as you are not going to let him get hurt.

With the dog either sitting or lying down at your side, with the lead slack, the dog recognises that you are in control and that there is no need for him to act defensively.

If you have been guilty of continually keeping your dog out of trouble when he exhibits aggressive behaviour, this could lead to him resenting others coming close to you, as you are his protector. The intervention of another person can threaten his security, which results in his being over-protective. He will resent anyone attempting to sit next to you and, either through aggression or persistent attention-seeking behaviour, will try to undermine the other person, until he removes himself.

Human nature being what it is, displays like this are often misinterpreted as the dog seemingly being devoted to you, which is very good for your ego. Because it appears that the dog wants you all to himself, you are inclined to tolerate the behaviour and, worse, condone it by getting the other person to move away. It is up to you to show the dog that, much as you love him, you will not tolerate such intervention between you and another person.

Sometimes, the dog is allowed to develop possessive feelings towards food, toys, furniture or territory.

It is a popular misconception that it is natural for a dog to growl at anyone who ventures near whilst he is eating his food or chewing on a bone. If the dog is permitted to get away with intimidating behaviour over something as important to him as food, he will almost certainly use aggression to achieve lesser goals.

The method described on page 69 when feeding puppies can be used just as effectively with an adult dog, and you must persist until the dog realises he only gets these things because you let him.

The more confident your approach when taking food or bones from him, the quicker he will respond in an acceptable fashion. Any display of possessiveness should be met with a very firm stare and an almost indignant attitude on your part – along the lines of, 'You are joking. Don't be so ridiculous,' said with a dismissive air. Don't give the food or bone back until the dog is obviously contrite over his actions.

The same method should be used if the dog shows possessive traits with his toys. He must be taught that he owns nothing and only has access to toys, etc., if you say so.

It is most important that you and other members of the family are consistent with permission and denials. For instance, if you do not want the dog to play with slippers, but another member of the family gives him a slipper to play with, this will confuse the dog over what is and is not acceptable behaviour. It will also undermine your authority with the dog, making future confrontations harder to deal with.

This also applies to territory and furniture. Either the dog is allowed on the settee or he is not. Either he is allowed in the bedrooms, or he is not. He must not be allowed by some members of the family, yet corrected for being there by others. He will become very confused by this and a confused dog is potentially an aggressive dog. You *can* train him, for example, that he is only allowed on the furniture when he is invited, but first he has to learn that he is only there because you say he can be.

Don't make the mistake of thinking that if others allow him to have, or do, things which you don't, that he will love them more and you less. A dog is much more secure when he knows exactly where his place is and is also much more secure when he can instantly recognise who is the leader of his 'pack'.

Finally in this category of incorrect basic training is the dog who has been allowed to mouth your hand or clothes, usually starting during puppyhood. Refer to Chapter 8, page 97 to overcome this problem.

Being Bitten by Another Dog
If your dog has been intimidated, attacked or bitten by another dog, he may make a point of avoiding that particular dog, dogs of that particular breed, or indeed all dogs. However, it can affect him the other way – he might actively want to attack that dog, breed type or all dogs.

Both these reactions are understandable and naturally you will have great sympathy with the dog's feelings. In the first instance, if you allow him to avoid the dog and over-protect him, you could actually make him more nervous. Of course, if the attacker is a known aggressive dog, not being properly controlled by the owner, it is common sense for you to avoid it and take whatever action you deem appropriate to prevent the situation happening again.

If it was just a one-off incident, over-protection by you will lead to him being even more wary. You will need to help the dog to regain his confidence, without 'babying' him. One of the best places to do this is at a dog training club where they teach modern, NON punishment orientated techniques and where the instructors have the proper experience and qualifications.

Leaving his Natural Mother at the Wrong Age

Sometimes, either through ignorance on the part of the breeder, or circumstances such as the bitch dying, puppies are taken from their natural mother too early. The ideal age for a pup to leave his mum is between seven to nine weeks, which is the crucial man-bonding time. Leaving mum and his litter brothers and sisters before this time means that he misses out on vital parts of his formative education and development.

The bitch teaches her pups what behaviour is acceptable, by admonishing them very firmly when they step out of line. She shows them, by example, how to interact with humans, what to be wary of and what things and situations are harmless.

Leaving his litter brothers and sisters too soon, he will not have completed learning the rules of behaviour when encountering other dogs. By play fighting in the litter, he learns how to moderate his behaviour so as not to cause discomfort, by experiencing early on what over-boisterous behaviour provokes in his litter mates. He learns the correct postures and signals to use when encountering another dog. If this learning is curtailed by leaving the litter before seven weeks old, he will not recognise these signals when he meets his first strange dog and may react in an aggressive fashion. Likewise, because *he* will be giving out confusing signals to the strange dog, that dog may act aggressively, because he is confused by the behaviour he is encountering.

This particularly applies when pups are orphaned at birth and hand-reared by humans. They tend to form a very deep attachment to the person who rears them, which in turn can lead to the pup being very possessive towards people. Not having had the benefit of another canine's teaching in proper dog behaviour, they are inclined to feel antagonistic towards other dogs, and will always relate closer to humans, perhaps finding other dogs a threat to that human relationship.

The reverse can happen if the pup stays with his mum too long, i.e. beyond nine weeks. Because he remains in a dog-oriented environment beyond the man-bonding time, he will relate more easily with dogs than with people, resulting in him being uneasy in human company, which could show itself as either very nervous behaviour or in displays of aggression.

If any of the above applies to your dog, you must pay great attention to socialising him, being scrupulously clear with your correction and reward. It would be very helpful if you could befriend someone who has a docile female dog, as she can help with showing your dog, in canine language, what behaviour is acceptable. Joining a dog training club could well help with finding a suitable companion for this purpose.

You may never achieve complete success in your attempts to mix your dog with other dogs and people, but you should achieve a level at which your dog can co-exist with both.

Poor Breeding
Although the majority of breeders are very selective, there are unfortunately many people who breed from unsuitable stock, often for very dubious reasons.

Some people breed from their bitch in the mistaken belief that it will 'be good for her to have a litter'. Even worse are those who breed from a bitch who has a poor temperament because they think it will improve it. Others breed simply with an eye to making money from the sale of the litter and, worst of all, are the puppy farmers, who over-breed their bitches, without giving a thought either to temperament, or to the health of the bitch or her pups.

Some of these people may well check the bitch and prospective stud dog for genetic faults, but do not give the same attention to the temperament of the prospective parents. Their offspring will inherit character traits from them both. Often the bitch is bred from far too early, without being given the chance to mature properly, either mentally or physically. As already mentioned, a bitch teaches her pups much by example and if she is nervous or immature, she will pass her own fears and phobias on to her offspring.

Inexperienced or ignorant breeders often fail to give correct advice to new owners when they ask for help, particularly when the owners find the dog showing character traits which they cannot understand. If poor breeding could be the reason why your dog is showing aggressive signs, you will need patience, positive training and the help of a good dog training club, to help you get the best from your dog.

Medical Ailments

You may have read all the categories previously mentioned, yet still cannot 'fit' your dog into any one of them, so cannot understand *why* your dog is being aggressive.

If this is the case, it would be advisable to have your dog thoroughly checked over by your veterinary surgeon. Simple things, such as ear infections, bad teeth, blocked anal glands, etc., can cause your dog to be bad tempered. Once treated, you may find that his aggressive behaviour ceases.

Unfortunately, there are more serious conditions, such as brain tumours, which cause the dog to act irrationally. Obviously in such cases, your vet is the best person qualified to give an opinion as to the dog's future.

Incorrect Diet

Some dogs can be so hyped up by the food they are being fed on that they become aggressive. It may be that the dog simply has an intolerance to a particular food, but often it can be attributed to additives in the food, or to being fed a completely inappropriate diet. See Chapter 6, Feeding Your Dog, page 57.

Dangerous Dogs

The final category which should be mentioned is the dog that has been specifically bred for fighting, and in some instances is actually *encouraged* to be aggressive. Of these dogs, the most notable is the American Pit Bull Terrier. Following a spate of attacks on people by these dogs, and also, it must be said, by some other breeds, the Dangerous Dogs Act 1991 and Dangerous Dogs (Amendment) Act 1997, passed in June 1997, was brought into force. Hopefully, none of the readers of this book will ever find themselves in possession of a truly vicious dog, but it is as well to know the outline of this Act. More details of the Act are given on page 200.

11

Neutering and Breeding

If you are not going to breed from your dog, it is generally better from both a behavioural and medical point of view to have him or her neutered.

Bitches – Spaying

A female dog will come into season usually every six months, starting at any time from five months of age, depending on breed and size. The season will last approximately three weeks, during which time she must be kept completely away from all male dogs. Some bitches will actively attempt to find a mate, so great care has to be taken to make sure she does not escape from the house or garden whilst she is in season.

Many bitches have what is known as a phantom pregnancy, where her head will tell her she is pregnant, even if she has not been anywhere near a male dog! She may show physical signs of pregnancy, such as producing milk and 'mothering' toys. She may undergo changes in temperament too, perhaps becoming snappy or possessive.

Physically, an unspayed bitch could be more prone to mammary tumours (like breast cancer in women) than a spayed bitch and older unspayed bitches are at risk of their womb becoming diseased, resulting in a possibly life-threatening condition called Pyometra (see Chapter 12, page 195).

Spaying will prevent any risk of pregnancy and stop her seasons. The operation involves a general anaesthetic and removal of the ovaries and womb. The bitch will have stitches which will be removed by your vet, usually after ten days. Until the stitches are removed, her exercise should be limited to gentle walks on the lead. Once the stitches are removed, she can return to normal exercise. You will need to watch her weight after she is spayed, as it can cause a slight metabolic change, which could lead to weight gain. Take advice from your vet to prevent this happening.

The best time to have your bitch spayed is after she has had her first season. Coming into season signifies that the bitch has matured, both mentally and physically. Although it is quite common nowadays to have bitches spayed before they have had a season, it can occasionally have a detrimental effect on the bitch from a psychological point of view – without going through the natural process of maturing and having that first season, some bitches can become mentally agitated when their season would normally have been due.

If the worst happens and your unspayed bitch does accidentally get mated, she can have what is call a misalliance injection. The injection is given on the third and fifth day after the mating, and will usually prevent her from having puppies on that occasion, although there is a small risk that the pregnancy will continue.

Males – Castration
The majority of male dogs are much easier to live with if they are castrated. They tend not to be aggressive to other males, and generally are more loving and compliant with their human family. There *are* people who assume that it will solve every training problem, which it won't – there is no replacement for basic training. It won't necessarily stop problems like territory marking, or indeed his knowing the difference between a dog or a bitch!

The operation stops the production of testosterone, the male hormone which tends to be at the root of aggression. It *does not* turn your male dog into a pathetic, weak animal, as some people believe, and, as previously mentioned, only changes his temperament *for the better*.

Although not such a big procedure as spaying, it is still done under a general anaesthetic. The dog will have stitches at the site from where the testicles have been removed, and you must ensure that the dog does not lick or bite the stitches. He will need restricted gentle exercise on the lead for a few days, or possibly until the stitches are removed by your vet, usually ten to fourteen days later. The dog will probably recover from the effects of the anaesthetic within twenty-four to forty-eight hours after the operation, and you will probably be surprised at how quickly the dog recovers generally – unlike humans, dogs do not feel sorry for themselves after surgery or injury, and seem to accept the situation remarkably quickly.

Again, as with bitches, you can have a male dog neutered when he is still a puppy, but my advice would be that, unless your dog has severe, sexually-based behavioural problems, it is best to wait until he is at least nine months old. It is my experience that, at whatever age the dog is when he is castrated, the mental maturing process tends to stop once the castration is done. You could therefore have a puppy castrated at four months old, and when he is, for example, two years old, he could still have the mental age of a four month old puppy!

Breeding
Breeding from a bitch, or using a male as a stud dog, should really be left to the knowledgeable expert. However, if you are thinking seriously about using your dog to breed from, you should at least have some idea of what you could be letting yourself in for.

Stud Dogs
If you own a male dog, you may feel that, as you won't be the one responsible for looking after any puppies, it is an easy way of making money, i.e. from stud fees.

What you should be aware of is how, once your dog has been used, his temperament may be changed forever. He may continually seek out other bitches whilst on exercise, refusing to return when called – the reproductive instinct is stronger than any other! He may well become aggressive with other male dogs, seeing them as a challenge to his supremacy. He may start mounting members of his human family, particularly the children.

If you are prepared for these possible changes in temperament, and decide to go ahead, you must first ensure that your dog is healthy, and does not have any genetic defects which he could pass on to his offspring. You should also have him tested to ensure that he does not carry any sexually transmitted disease, which could be passed on to the bitch during mating. Even if the dog has not been used for stud before, he could still be carrying infection, which could affect both the conception of, and viability of, any subsequent puppies. Temperamentally, he should be neither aggressive nor shy, as both these traits could be passed on to the puppies. As the stud dog owner, you must be prepared to 'entertain' the bitch and her owner in your home, when the time for mating arrives. This may last for several hours and usually requires two visits, so that the bitch can be mated twice. If you have children in the house, they should be kept well away in case of any aggression – quite often the bitch will be snappy to begin with, and you certainly would not want to risk the children getting bitten.

Having already mentioned stud fees, it may well turn out that even after two visits from the bitch, she does not get pregnant, and therefore you will not receive a stud fee.

Overall, stud dog ownership is not as simple as it first appears. It really is best to leave it to the experts – and after all, there are already thousands of unwanted dogs in this country, which you could be adding to if you allow your dog to be used.

Bitches

Even in this supposedly enlightened age, there is still the widely held myth that it is good for a bitch to have at least one litter of puppies. There is no scientific or medical evidence to back this up, whereas there have been many cases of bitches suffering medical problems, either during the birth of the puppies, or shortly afterwards.

Although it could be said that giving birth is a natural process, humans have interfered so much in the dog world that there are some breeds that have been altered by selective breeding to the extent that they cannot give birth naturally. One instance of this is with the Bulldog – the head of the Bulldog has been developed to be so large that the puppies' heads are too big to pass naturally through the birth canal and therefore puppies have to be born by caesarean section.

In a worst case scenario, you may lose both bitch and puppies due to birthing complications, and, apart from the distress this would cause, it would also involve huge veterinary bills.

If you are determined to breed from your bitch, you should first wait until she is at least two years old, and then have her checked for any genetic defects which she could pass on to her puppies. You should also have had her tested to ensure that she is not carrying any sexually transmitted disease or infection which she may pass on to the stud dog during mating – indeed many owners of stud dogs will insist upon this. A maiden bitch could still carry infection, such as Beta Haemolytic Strep or Pasteurella, which could be passed on to the stud dog during mating. You should only breed from her if her temperament is sound. As she is the one who rears the puppies, any character defects may be passed on to her puppies, as they will learn from her example. You will also need to choose the stud dog carefully, making sure that he too has been checked for any defects, and also that he is sound in temperament. She will need to be treated for worms before she is mated, to minimise the quantity of worms which she will pass on to her unborn puppies.

Assuming your bitch becomes pregnant, you will need to ensure that she is fed the correct amounts as her pregnancy proceeds. Towards the end of the pregnancy, she may be eating more than twice her normal quantity of food. She will still need gentle exercise on the lead, to keep her body fit and supple, but you will also need to keep her away from any possible infection, to protect her and her unborn puppies.

You must have the room, time and money to be able to house and rear the puppies properly. You are also responsible for finding good homes for all of them, and providing back-up help for the new owners. Initially, the bitch will keep her puppies and the whelping area clean, but, once the puppies start to be weaned, they will pass copious amounts of urine and faeces and it can be a very dirty business which needs clearing up frequently! Weaning a litter on to solid food is also a very time consuming, messy and expensive affair.

The puppies will need worming before they go to their new homes, and responsible breeders will provide veterinary insurance for the puppies for at least the first four to six weeks after they have gone to their new home. You should also provide the new owners with a copy of the pedigree certificate (where appropriate), a registration and transfer of ownership document (again if appropriate) and written details of the diet and care that the new puppy will need.

You may get extremely attached to the puppies and find it very upsetting when they go to their new homes. You also have to be prepared to take back any puppies if the new owners decide they cannot cope with or care for them.

Hopefully you will decide that dog breeding should be left to the experts who have the expertise and facilities to do the job properly.

12

Keeping Your Dog Healthy

Hopefully, your dog will lead a long and healthy life. A few sensible precautions on your part will increase the chances of your dog doing just that. You also have a responsibility to ensure that your dog does not spread disease to other dogs or indeed to humans.

General
Regular Inoculations
With the system currently in operation in this country, killer diseases which can affect dogs have been closely controlled and in some cases almost eradicated.

The most lethal of them all, rabies, has been so far excluded from the UK and Ireland by the quarantine laws. Quarantine means long separation from our dogs, which is not very pleasant, but it is infinitely better than bringing in a disease which could have such awful consequences on domestic animals, wild life and humans. It is up to all of us to act responsibly to ensure that rabies never reaches this country and to report any known instances of quarantine evasion to the authorities immediately. (See also page 191.)

Fortunately, the quarantine laws for Great Britain have been partially changed, with the introduction of the Pet Travel Scheme also known as Passports for Pets. See page 201 for more details of this scheme.

The four main diseases which can be controlled by regular inoculation are Distemper, Hepatitis, Leptospirosis and Parvo Virus. This last disease, Parvo Virus, is relatively new. It particularly affects young puppies and elderly dogs and is quite virulent in some parts of the country.

All dogs must be inoculated against these diseases, to lessen even further the chance of an epidemic. Puppies are usually inoculated at around eight weeks and again at twelve weeks. After that, yearly booster inoculations are advised, so that the dog has continual protection throughout his life. Until puppies have received their second inoculation at twelve weeks, they should not be mixed with other dogs. You can also have your dog inoculated against kennel cough, which should be done twice yearly (see page 195).

There is some research being done which is indicating that perhaps it is not necessary to give dogs booster vaccinations every year and in fact it may even be counter productive to do so. However, be guided by your veterinary surgeon.

Worming
Your dog should be treated for the prevention of worms at least twice a year – more often if your dog is a scavenger. There are two main groups of worms which affect dogs – roundworms and tapeworms. Worm infestation can cause abnormal hunger, diarrhoea, poor growth, itching around the bottom and general loss of condition.

Untreated dogs can pass worms on to other dogs, via the eggs which are deposited in the faeces when the dog goes to the toilet. The eggs are then moved around by the wind and on the soles of people's shoes, or by sticking to the feet of passing dogs. That dog then licks himself and ingests the eggs, causing the dog to becoming infested.

An unwormed dog could also cause a disease in humans called Visceral Larva Migrans, which is caused by ingesting the egg of the roundworm Toxocara Canis. Children are particularly at risk, as they tend to put their hands near or into their mouths, especially if they should do so after touching a piece of ground infected with the worm eggs, or if they are petting a dog who has worms. The egg can enter via contact from hand to mouth, and, in very severe cases, can cause blindness or mental retardation. Although these cases are rare, simple precautions such as always washing your hands after handling a dog, particularly a strange dog, and ensuring that your dog is regularly treated for worms, will prevent this from happening. It is worth noting that unwormed cats carry a similar worm – Toxocara Cati – which can also cause the same disease in humans as Toxocara Canis.

You must treat your dog for worms, even if you never see any actual evidence – the eggs which pass from the dog via the faeces are minute. If you should see what appear to be small grains of rice in the faeces and around the anal area, that is very clear evidence that your dog has a severe infestation of tapeworms. If you see what look like strands of spaghetti in the faeces or vomit, you can be sure that your dog has a roundworm infestation.

There is also a strain of tapeworm, which, if ingested during its development stage, can affect humans, causing a disease called Hydatidosis, which affects the liver and lungs. Fortunately, cases of this disease are extremely rare.

All this unpleasantness can be avoided if all dog owners abide by the following simple rules:

1. All puppies should be wormed before leaving the breeder, at three weeks and five weeks of age. They should be wormed again twice more by the time they reach 13 weeks. Thereafter they should be regularly wormed every six months throughout their lives. Get the worm prevention treatment from your veterinary surgeon – tablets and powders from the pet shop are not as effective.

2. Bitches who are about to be bred from should be wormed prior to mating and again after the puppies are weaned.

3. All faeces should be removed daily from the garden and burned or hygienically disposed of. Always remove any faeces your dog leaves behind when out on exercise.

4. Always wash your hands after handling your dog, before consuming food.

By following these simple procedures, you can be assured that you have taken all possible steps to prevent your dog passing the infection to other dogs or humans.

Fleas
All dogs are extremely susceptible to fleas (as indeed are cats). Fleas can be seen quickly moving over the dog's skin and are particularly partial to the base of the dog's tail and behind his ears. Flea droppings look like specks of grit and are especially visible on the dog's stomach.

Dog fleas are quite indiscriminate and will infest the clean, healthy dog just as much as the dirty, neglected animal. Flea bites can cause extreme irritation to the dog. Some dogs also become allergic to the saliva which is injected into the skin when the flea bites. As well as the irritation caused, fleas are also the intermediate host of the tapeworm.

At one time, flea infestations were confined to the warmer summer months but nowadays, with more and more homes being centrally heated, that is no longer true. Fleas like warmth and will lay their eggs in the gap between the carpet and the skirting board, between the floorboards, in the pile of fitted carpets and in the dog's bedding and basket. After the eggs hatch, the larvae stage can remain dormant for anything up to one year if the temperature is not warm enough, before jumping onto the next passing host – perhaps your dog or, worse still, you! – for a meal.

Fleas do not live on the dog, but simply use him as a source of food. They will live in your home, and anywhere where the dog regularly goes, such as the car.

Only fastidious attention to flea control will ensure that your dog is kept clear of these prolific parasites. There are many different types of flea prevention products available from your vet, and he or she can advise you on the most suitable for your particular needs.

You must treat the home and car regularly in order to kill off the larvae and any adult fleas. As fleas like warm areas, you need to pay special attention to those areas in your home, such as the carpet beneath the radiators, the settee, and the bedroom. Do remember to treat all pet bedding too. If you only treat the animal, without doing the animal's environment, you will be leaving all the eggs to hatch out and re-infect the animal.

One of the best ways to prevent fleas getting a hold in your home is regular use of the vacuum cleaner. This will suck up the eggs around the edges of the carpets, before they have a chance to hatch.

Stings

Bee and wasp stings can cause the same reaction in dogs as they do in humans. More often it is young puppies who are fascinated by the movement and buzzing sound and either try to sniff at them or catch them in their mouths. Either action can result in the puppy being stung.

If stung in the mouth, head or neck area, seek veterinary assistance as the area will swell and could compromise the dog's breathing.

If the dog is stung on the foot, perhaps by treading on the wasp or bee, and, provided that the dog shows no sign of allergic reaction (such as distress and collapse), you should be able to treat the sting yourself. Bathe the area with vinegar for a wasp sting or with bicarbonate of soda for a bee sting. If in any doubt, contact your vet.

Ticks

Although not as common as the flea, dogs can get ticks even if they live in the town. Hedgehogs carry these parasites, as well as farm animals. Adult ticks live on the host, sucking the blood, then fall off and lay their eggs. The eggs attach themselves to grasses and branches, and wait for the next host to pass by, when they attach themselves, and the cycle starts again.

You may well not notice the tick to begin with, and it is only when the tick begins to grow that you will see a wart-like swelling on the dog, which can grow up to 1cm as it engorges with blood.

Ticks are usually found on the legs, chest, neck or face. DON'T be tempted to pull it off – if you do, you will probably leave the mouth parts behind, which may become infected and cause an abscess. Your vet can remove the whole tick safely. Ticks can also transmit disease to humans.

Lice

Less common than either the flea or tick, lice can infest the run down or stray dog. There are two types – those which bite and feed off dead skin, and sucking lice which feed from the blood of the dog. Flea prevention products (available from your veterinary surgeon) should also prevent this unpleasant parasite from invading your dog.

Snake Bites

In the British Isles we are fortunate that there is only one poisonous snake – the adder. This is a protected species, and generally causes humans little or no problem, as the adder prefers to keep out of our way.

In warm weather the adder likes to come above ground to bask in the sunshine. Usually, the vibrations caused by our footsteps warn the adder of our approach and it will quickly disappear. Unfortunately dogs, being lighter and more inquisitive of areas off the beaten track, do occasionally get bitten, usually on the foot, lower leg, chest, neck or nose.

You may not be immediately aware if your dog does get bitten. Sometimes he may yelp, but it could be that the first sign is either a swelling where the dog has been bitten, or you may indeed not notice anything until the dog collapses.

If you can avoid making the dog walk, so much the better – any exertion will accelerate the blood circulation, which in turn will quicken the spread of the venom through the dog's system.

If you can't carry the dog, walk him calmly to the car, keeping calm yourself so as not to cause the dog any more distress. Seek veterinary assistance immediately.

Day-to-Day Care
Grooming
Whether your dog has a short or long coat, he should be brushed regularly to keep his coat healthy, clean and tangle-free. The shorter-coated dog should be brushed at least once a week, whilst the dog with a longer coat needs brushing daily to keep it in tip-top condition. A few minutes spent every day is far better than half an hour once a week.

When you are brushing your dog, it is also a good time to check him over and examine him for any cuts, bumps or sores (see Chapter 7, page 72).

Bathing
It is really a personal choice as to how often you bath your dog, but regular brushing should be sufficient most of the time. Obviously, if your dog has rolled in something unpleasant, or during a heavy moult, a bath may be necessary. It is also a good idea to bath a bitch once she has finished her season, to get rid of any 'interesting' smells which may remain. On these occasions, do use a proper, good-quality dog shampoo and rinse the coat thoroughly.

Where possible, bath your dog on a warm, sunny day, so that after you have removed the excess water with a towel, your dog can stay outside and dry his coat properly. If it is a cold or wet day, dry as much as possible with a towel, then use a hair drier, or let him lie in front of a warm, but not hot, fire. Make sure that his joints are dried thoroughly, to prevent any future problems with rheumatism.

Swimming
Many dogs enjoy swimming and it can be very good exercise for them. If you do allow your dog into the sea, you must rinse his coat well in fresh water when you return home, as the salt and the sand can cause skin irritation. Also, please be considerate if you take your dog onto the beach. It can be very annoying for other beach users to have a dog running through their possessions and having to avoid the little 'piles' which dogs can leave behind them!

Exercise
It is impossible to generalise over how much exercise you should give your dog. Some need a five-mile walk daily, whilst others only need a short run around the park.

As a very rough guide, medium to large breeds such as Alsatians, Retrievers, Labradors, Collies, etc., should have at least one *good* walk every day, supplemented with shorter walks on the lead.

The very large heavy breeds, such as Newfoundlands, Pyreneans and St. Bernards, should not be run for miles and miles – they are quite content to have shorter, more sedate regular exercise, although they can walk a fair distance at a gentle pace.

With the smaller breeds, it very much depends on the type of dog – some small dogs can run for hours, whilst others can only take exercise in short bursts. Find out from the breeder, or the vet, exactly how much your particular dog should have.

If you have re-homed an adult dog, then you can start taking him out immediately, provided he has had all the usual vaccinations. The amount of exercise the dog will need should be appropriate for the size and age of the dog. As mentioned at the beginning, it is wrong to assume that a small dog such as a Jack Russell Terrier will not need as much exercise as a German Shepherd Dog, for example. Obviously, *all* dogs should be taken out *at least* once a day, preferably more, and at least one of those daily walks should be off-the-lead exercise. Depending on the time you have available, all dogs will benefit from at least an hour off-the-lead exercise daily.

With young puppies, once they are allowed out, the exercise should be modified according to the size of dog they will eventually become. A common mistake is for new owners of the larger breeds to assume that the puppies can take more exercise, as they grow so rapidly. With the larger breeds, the puppies *are* growing quickly, and as such their bones can be easily damaged by too much strenuous exercise. The smaller breeds still need to take it carefully to begin with, even though they don't have so much growing to do.

Teeth

A dog has 42 teeth when fully grown – 12 incisors, 4 canines, 16 premolars, 4 upper molars and 6 lower molars.

Puppies have usually lost all their milk teeth by around six months old. Occasionally a milk tooth may be retained, even though the adult tooth has grown alongside. This can sometimes cause the puppy to continue destructive chewing, as he did when the adult teeth started coming through. The retained milk tooth (or teeth) will probably need to be removed, by your vet.

The right diet, as described in Chapter 6, page 59, will greatly assist in keeping tooth disease at bay. Additionally, cleaning the teeth, especially the canines, which are not involved in the ripping and tearing action, will help prevent decay and gum disease.

Canine toothpaste and brushes can be obtained from your vet and if you start cleaning the teeth from puppyhood, your dog will accept that this is part of his regular grooming routine. Start by putting a small spot of toothpaste on your finger and gently rub your finger over the dog's teeth. After doing this a few times, you can progress to using the brush. Although time-consuming, if you can clean the dog's teeth at least two or three times a week, you may well prevent expensive dental treatment in the future and save your dog from the discomfort of gingivitis (inflamed gums) or tooth decay.

Dental problems may be slow to detect. You may notice the dog choosing not to eat hard food, having unpleasant smelling breath, or salivating more than usual. Left for too long, the dog will start to lose weight. Early detection of gum or teeth disorders may save your dog from permanently losing some teeth, so regular inspection of the dog's mouth and teeth is strongly advised.

Diseases Transmittable to Humans from Dogs

Having previously mentioned how the presence of worms in your dog could, in rare instances, affect humans, there are other conditions that can transfer from dogs to humans. One of these is *Sarcoptic Mange*, which is a skin condition caused by a mite which burrows through the skin. In the dog, this results in fur loss and skin irritation and, when it is passed to humans, the mite can cause a transient skin disorder. Although not life-threatening, it can be most unpleasant and will need medical attention. Obviously, the dog will also require veterinary treatment.

Ringworm

Although the name of this condition suggests it is caused by a worm, it is in fact a fungal infection, similar to athlete's foot, and is contagious to humans. It affects the skin, and is seen as a ring shape, causing the skin to itch and redden and affecting the hair cells. This condition, though unpleasant, is not life-threatening and responds well to treatment.

Rabies

Having previously mentioned the quarantine laws currently in force, it is to be hoped that we never see the effect that this awful virus can have on mankind. The infection is passed from rabid animals (not just dogs) via the animal's saliva, usually through a bite, but occasionally the saliva can be transmitted via a pre-existing skin wound. It then attacks the nervous system and subsequently enters the brain. The condition is invariably fatal in both animals and man.

Common Ailments and Infectious Diseases

The following section deals with the more common illnesses and afflictions which you may encounter with your dog. It is NOT intended to be a self-help guide to treating your dog. *Always seek veterinary advice whenever your dog is showing signs of illness or discomfort.*

Anal Glands

The anal glands are two small scent glands, one on either side of the anus, just underneath the tail. The glands contain a very strong smelling substance, which the dog can expel after defecation, either to mark his territory, or when he is feeling very fearful. Some dogs can have problems with these glands, and they may need emptying from time to time – a procedure which is definitely one to leave for your vet to perform. Occasionally abscesses may form in the glands, or they can become impacted. You may notice the dog appearing to 'slide' along on his bottom, as he attempts to relieve the irritation of the impacted glands. If the dog continues to have problems with these glands, they can be surgically removed.

Cystitis

This is an infection in the bladder and causes the dog to pass frequent small amounts of urine, which may contain specks of blood. It is more common in bitches, but can affect males too. Treatment with antibiotics is required, and if you suspect that your dog may have cystitis, try to take a fresh sample of the dog's urine with you when you take him or her to the vet. By testing the urine, the vet will be able to make a positive diagnosis, and treatment can start immediately.

Care should be taken to prevent urine scald around the urinary opening. Bathing the area with warm water, careful drying and then applying calendula powder will help both prevent and relieve the scalding.

Diarrhoea

An upset tummy can be an indication of many conditions, including worms, bacterial infection, viruses, allergic reaction to food, or poisoning. Withhold all food immediately, but ensure the dog has access to water. It may be simply a 'one off' caused perhaps by something the dog has eaten which disagrees with him. Provided there is no blood in the diarrhoea, and the dog is showing no other signs of illness, starving him for 24 hours should sort his tummy out. If he is still passing runny motions after 24 hours, seek veterinary advice. Once diagnosis and treatment are complete, it is often helpful to give your dog a daily spoonful of plain, live yoghurt – this will help replenish the friendly natural gut bacteria. Feed a light diet for a few days, such as cooked chicken and rice, or cooked fish and rice.

Ear Infections

Signs of ear problems can range from increased warmth of the ear on touching, sensitivity of the area, drooping ears, holding the head to one side, scratching at the ears, a discharge from the ear, or continual shaking of the head. This could be due to ear mites, an ear infection, a trapped grass seed, or a foreign body stuck in the ear. *Do not attempt to treat by poking anything in the ear or administering any liquid into the ear*. You could permanently damage the ear and the hearing. Consult your vet for diagnosis and treatment.

Eclampsia

This condition affects bitches who have just had puppies, either soon after the birth or during the nursing stages, but occasionally it may happen just before the bitch whelps. It is caused by a reduced level of calcium in the blood, normally due to the demands of the nursing puppies on the bitch, which depletes her supply. Signs could be some or all of the following: loss of appetite, high fever, possibly convulsions, restlessness, panting, nervousness, stiffness, muscular spasms or twitching. Immediate veterinary treatment is essential, as this condition is life-threatening.

Eyes

One of the more common ailments which can affect the dog's eyes is conjunctivitis. It is typified by a pale greeny-white discharge at the inner corner of one or both eyes, and the eyes may look sore and red. Early treatment from your vet, either with an antibiotic cream or drops, will quickly clear up this condition.

More serious eye conditions, such as cataracts or entropion, usually need surgery to rectify them. Cataracts can affect dogs in the same way as they can affect people, and are more commonly seen in the older dog. The lens has a cloudy appearance, and the dog will possibly be showing signs of not seeing clearly. Entropion is a condition where the eyelid turns inwards and, as a result, the eyelashes then come into contact with the surface of the eye, rubbing against the eye and causing ulceration. This condition is often inherited, and there is a screening system available, where owners can have future breeding stock checked to see if they carry this condition. Occasionally, entropion can develop after frequent bouts of conjunctivitis, especially if the conjunctivitis remains untreated for long periods.

Heatstroke

Most dogs do not enjoy being exposed to hot sun. Their body temperature is higher than ours – between 38.3°

and 38.7° Centigrade – and as such they feel the heat more than we do. Add to that the addition of a thick fur coat and the very limited ability to dissipate heat – by panting and through the pads under their feet – and you can see how dogs will suffer in hot weather. During the summer months, it is best to restrict the dog to light exercise during the heat of the day, leaving strenuous exercise either for early morning or evening. Make sure they always have access to both shade and water.

If your dog is unfortunate enough to suffer from heatstroke, there are some immediate first-aid procedures you can perform. Signs of heatstroke are panting, profuse salivation, vomiting and general weakness. Remove the dog to an area of shade, preferably where there is a breeze, and apply ice packs and/or cold water to the head, neck and shoulder area. If the dog is able to drink, offer him *small* quantities of water at regular intervals. Continue the treatment and seek veterinary help immediately.

Never leave a dog unattended in a car during warm weather. Every year, there are reports of dogs dying in cars – the owners may only have left them for a few minutes but, even with the windows open, cars can become ovens in minutes, causing dogs extreme distress, which can lead very quickly to collapse and death. I did an experiment with my own car, to see what the temperature was inside, on a hot, sunny day. The car, an estate, was parked on the roadside, with a small amount of shade being cast on it. The outside temperature was 80° Fahrenheit.

With all the windows fully opened, the sunroof and the tailgate open, after ten minutes the temperature inside the car was the same as outside, i.e. 80°.

With the windows half open, the sunroof open and the tailgate shut (as you may possibly leave the car when popping into a shop), within ten minutes the temperature inside the car was 98°.

With windows, sunroof and tailgate all shut, the temperature inside the car reached 122° within ten minutes. So, you can see that even with leaving windows opened, the dog would very quickly be overcome. It is not just the heat that kills, but also the lack of air circulation – **don't take the risk!**

Kennel Cough

Despite implication from the name, kennel cough can be contracted anywhere, not just in kennels. It is a condition caused by one or more of several agents – bacteria, virus and mycoplasma – spread by droplet, and extremely contagious. The cough is usually harsh, as if something is stuck in the throat. Sometimes there is also a clear, watery discharge from the eyes and nose, and the dog may appear to be a little fussy over food. Veterinary advice should be taken, as antibiotics may be needed to prevent secondary infection in the chest. A teaspoonful of clear honey given at regular intervals will help soothe the throat, as will a spoonful of low-fat vanilla ice-cream. Your dog will need to be kept away from other dogs all the time he is still coughing, and for two weeks following cessation of coughing, as he could still be infectious. Your vet can advise you about vaccinating your dog against kennel cough.

Pyometra

This is a condition which only affects unspayed bitches and is an infection of the uterus. It is a condition which requires urgent veterinary attention and, if left untreated, the bitch will probably die. More commonly it occurs soon after the bitch has been in season. The onset can be quite sudden – vomiting, diarrhoea, discoloured vaginal discharge, loss of appetite and excessive thirst and urination – some or all of these symptoms may be present. Occasionally a bitch will have a closed pyometra, where the infection remains enclosed in the uterus, and therefore there is no external evidence of a discharge. Sometimes the bitch will display similar symptoms as described above, but also may just appear to be generally lethargic, off her food and with a raised temperature. Urgent treatment is still needed. In both cases, immediate removal of the womb is the only treatment.

Skin Conditions

There is a veritable myriad of skin conditions, ranging from flea allergies, food allergies, contact allergies, mange, ringworm, eczema and so on. They can manifest themselves in a variety of ways: dry skin, flaky skin, redness, itching, greasy hair, pimples, scabs, hair loss, foul-smelling skin. Indeed, canine skin problems are now one of the biggest reasons why dogs visit the vet. All skin conditions need prompt attention, so don't leave it in the hope that it will clear itself up – it won't! It is important to know that two of these skin conditions are transmittable to humans.

MANGE

Demodectic mange is caused by a microscopic mite that lives in the hair follicles. This cannot be passed on to humans, but sarcoptic mange, which is caused by a mite which burrows into the skin, *is* contagious to humans.

RINGWORM

Ringworm is caused by a fungus, not a worm. It grows on the skin, starting at a centre point and growing outwards in a ring shape. As it grows, the hair and skin become thickened and irritated, and the hair sometimes breaks. Ringworm is contagious to humans.

Torsion – Acute Gastric Dilation

This is an extremely serious condition, which, if undetected or left untreated, can result in death within a few hours of onset. It tends to be a condition more commonly associated with the larger, deeper chested breeds, and can occur shortly after the dog has eaten, due to excess gas production or gas which is unable to escape. This causes distension of the stomach, which in turn causes impaired blood flow. The dog will show signs of distress, salivate profusely, show an enlarged abdomen and attempt to vomit. Left untreated, the dog will go into shock, and ultimately collapse and die. URGENT veterinary help is required. A further complication is when the stomach then rotates and twists (torsion), which usually requires emergency surgery.

Although the cause of gastric dilation is not completely understood, there are one or two things you can do to help prevent it recurring. To reduce the amount of air intake when your dog is feeding, place the bowl in a feeding stand, approximately at shoulder height to the dog. Instead of feeding the dog twice a day, feed three or four smaller meals. Restrict the amount of water the dog takes in at any one time – obviously the dog needs to drink, but don't allow him copious amounts all in one go.

Vomiting

If a dog is being sick repeatedly, it could well be just one symptom of any number of different illnesses. It may be something as simple as an upset stomach, or it could be an indication of much more serious problems, such as poisoning, kidney problems or an allergic reaction to drug treatment. If the dog is sick just once, and appears to be perfectly well in every other way, it may simply be something that he has scavenged which has caused him to vomit. Often, dogs will deliberately cause themselves to vomit, usually by first eating grass (a natural emetic), which will prompt the elimination of bile.

Obviously, if the dog is being sick, plus showing other signs of being unwell, a trip to the vet is needed.

The above are just a few of the illnesses and conditions which you may encounter at some time throughout your dog's lifetime. With common sense and by taking the right precautions, plus guidance from your veterinary surgeon, you should be able to reduce substantially any risk to your dog from illness or disease.

Although any ailment or illness should always be

checked out with your vet, it is a good idea to have a simple canine first-aid kit, for use in the case of minor ailments. **Check with your vet first, before treating any condition yourself**. As a suggestion, the kit should comprise bandages, veterinary wound powder (an antiseptic powder for cuts or bites) and liquid paraffin (for aiding the digestive system if your dog is constipated).

Homeopathic and Bach Flower Remedies

Many dog owners and some vets now use a variety of alternative therapies for treating some medical conditions which haven't responded well to conventional medicine. Homeopathic and Bach Flower remedies are just two of the alternatives which may be tried at home, particularly for minor ailments. You could add the following to your first-aid kit: arnica (a homeopathic remedy for sore joints or as an aid to post-operative healing), rescue remedy (a Bach Flower remedy for the treatment of stress or nerves), calendula powder and cream (a very useful soothing remedy for stings, bites, sores etc), and finally a homeopathic snake bite remedy, available from homeopathic pharmacies, for the immediate treatment of adder bites.

Always take veterinary advice before you treat the dog yourself.

13

The Law and Your Dog

Identification
It is a legal requirement that your dog wear a collar carrying a visible means of identifying you as his owner. Even if your dog is microchipped or tattooed, he must still wear this identification.

Dogs on Leads
When walking along any road, your dog must be held on a lead. No matter how well-trained your dog becomes, he can still be spooked by a loud noise or unfamiliar object and, if you are foolish enough to allow him to be walking free, he could well end up darting into the road, perhaps causing a serious accident in the process. As the person in charge of the dog, you will be held liable for any such accident, and you may well end up responsible for repairs to cars and/or property – and possible personal injury claims too.

Children Exercising Dogs
Although not yet enforceable by law, it is very irresponsible to allow unsupervised children to take a dog out. Dogs are unpredictable – all manner of things can change your placid pooch into an angry, aggressive or defensive dog. A child does not have the ability or knowledge to cope with that type of occurrence. Children are not only unpredictable themselves sometimes, but are also not physically strong enough to hold a dog if he decides to 'take off'. This doesn't just apply to the

larger breeds either – often the smaller dogs are more highly strung and just as likely to be frightened or goaded into unusual behaviour.

Picking Up After Your Dog
Nearly all public parks and outside recreational spaces are now designated as 'pick-up' areas, as well as all pavements and grass verges. You should always carry either a plastic bag or poop-scoop and, once collected, the waste matter should either be deposited in one of the specified dog waste bins, or, if not available, the waste should be taken home and disposed of hygienically. Failure to clean up after your dog could make you liable to a fine of anything up to £1,000.

The Dangerous Dogs Act
This Act does not just apply to Pit Bull Terriers, or large breeds such as German Shepherd Dogs or Rottweilers. It applies to ALL dogs. Furthermore, your dog need not necessarily have bitten someone for you to be summonsed under the Act. As a dog owner, you are responsible for your dog's actions and, more importantly, how those actions are perceived by other people. *You* may know that your big friendly Labrador is only charging across the park to say, 'Hello,' to the person on the other side. That person, however, who may not even have a dog with him, sees a dog hurtling towards him and may well be very fearful, scared that your dog is going to attack them. He could see the dog as being out of control and you could be prosecuted as a result. Worse still, if he is so scared that he starts to shout, or run away, that may well prompt your dog to jump at him, or to cause the dog to act out of character.

It is up to you to ensure that your dog never causes a nuisance to others, however well-intentioned the dog's actions may be. The Act can be enforced against any breed of dog which is deemed to be dangerously out of control in a public place. Even if the dog has not injured anyone, if there are grounds to believe that he *may* do so, all or any of the following restrictions may be enforced:

- The dog may be destroyed.
- The owner is liable for a fine, a term of imprisonment, or both.
- The owner may be disqualified from keeping a dog, for such a period as the court deems fit.

You can see therefore how important it is that your dog is properly trained and controlled at all times.

Quarantine (see also Chapter 12, page 181)

After many years of discussion, the rules on quarantine have been partially changed. Quarantine has not been abolished altogether, and dogs entering the UK from most countries still have to spend six months in quarantine kennels.

Pet Passports

A new pilot Pet Travel Scheme (PETS), also known as Passport for Pets, has been introduced. Under the scheme, pet dogs and cats **resident in the UK** may visit the countries listed below and return without the need for quarantine. Dogs and cats travelling under the scheme that **come** from the following countries, and have been resident there at least for six months, may enter the UK without going into quarantine, provided they have shown a negative blood test for rabies at least six months before they travel. The countries are: Andorra, Austria, Belgium, Denmark, Finland, France, Germany, Gibraltar, Greece, Iceland, Italy, Liechtenstein, Luxembourg, Monaco, the Netherlands, Norway, Portugal, San Marino, Spain, Sweden, Switzerland and the Vatican. Within some of these countries, there are certain areas which are excluded, so it is advisable to check with DEFRA (the Department for Environment, Food and Rural Affairs) before embarking on any travel plans. Only certain air and sea routes into and out of the UK are operating under PETS, so you will need to check this with your travel operator.

Under PETS, dogs and cats from the Channel Islands, the Isle of Man and the Republic of Ireland can go to any qualifying country and return to the UK, provided they have the official certification. Jersey, Guernsey, the Isle of Man and the Republic of Ireland have each produced their own official PETS certificate.

The criteria for travelling to the countries listed above **from** the UK is as follows:

1. The dog must be fitted with a permanent number microchip – your own vet can do this.

2. The dog must have been vaccinated against rabies, using an approved vaccine – your own vet can do this at the time of microchipping. (The dog must also have booster vaccinations at required intervals.) Dogs under three months old cannot be vaccinated.

3. Thirty days after vaccination, the dog must have a blood test to check that the required antibody levels have been achieved. The blood has to be tested by a laboratory approved by DEFRA. If the required levels are not achieved, the dog must be re-vaccinated and the blood tested after another thirty days. **IMPORTANT: Your dog cannot re-enter the UK until six months after the date that the blood sample was taken which led to a successful test result.**

4. The dog must have a health certificate certifying that the above criteria has been met. This certificate must be signed by an approved Local Veterinary Inspector.

5. The dog must have been treated for certain parasites and ticks 24 to 48 hours before the dog enters the UK. The dog must also have a certificate from an official vet stating that these treatments have been given. (You will need to find a vet in the country you are visiting who has the right medication and documentation.)

Although not part of the conditions, it would also be advisable to keep to your regular flea prevention routine and ensure your dog has been treated with an appropriate flea/tick product *before* leaving this country – this will then protect your dog from ticks whilst you are abroad. Only treating the dog before your return to this country will not cover the dog during your stay abroad, where he is open to infestation from ticks not found in the UK, and he could be gestating tick bite fever, without showing any signs, before the required check by a vet 24 to 48 hours before you return home. Tick bites can cause a disease called Babesia Canis, which can prove fatal, and ticks can transmit potentially serious diseases to both pets and humans, such as Babesiosis and Ehrlichiosis. Make sure the dog is protected BEFORE you travel. It would also be advisable to check with your vet about specified diseases which may be prevalent in the country you are planning to visit, but which do not occur in the UK. Your dog will not have built up any immunity to such diseases, and your vet may be able to provide preventative treatment.

Failure to adhere to any of these conditions may render the Pet Passport invalid and the dog would have to go into quarantine for six months. Any vet can microchip, vaccinate and take blood for testing, but only approved laboratories can carry out the blood test, and only Local Veterinary Inspectors are able to issue pet health certificates.

For dogs leaving the UK, owners should also check to see if they need a separate health certificate to show that the dog meets the health requirements of the country they are visiting. The PETS system is continually under review and it would be advisable to check with DEFRA and/or your vet for any changes which may have been implemented since the writing of this book.

14

Caring for the Ageing Dog

Not unlike humans, as a dog ages his requirements for sleep, food and exercise will change. He may develop some hearing loss, or his eyesight may deteriorate. His joints may start to stiffen and his appetite may become a little delicate. Depending on the size and breed of your dog, changes due to ageing can start any time from as early as five years old. Continued exercise is important, but should be adapted to his ability. Take advice from your veterinary surgeon about altering the dog's food. You may well need to change his diet, either to a proprietary 'senior' dog food, or perhaps pandering to him a little and giving him cooked chicken or fish.

As the dog ages, he must be allowed to spend more time resting, and should be protected from unwanted attention from either children or other pets. He may become a little irritable as he gets older, and will not show the same patience with youngsters as he did in his youth. He may start to dislike being left alone, so perhaps employing a dog-sitter should be considered. As time goes on, he may not be able to control his bladder or bowels quite so well, so will need more frequent trips to the garden, and may have the odd accident indoors.

Frequently, as the dog ages, people think about getting another puppy, perhaps to give the older dog a 'new lease of life'. In my experience, I have always found this to be very beneficial for both older dog and puppy alike, as the older dog tends to start to play again, with the puppy, and the pup can sometimes learn from the older, wiser dog. Of course, you must make sure that the puppy does not worry the older dog, and the pup must be trained to leave the older dog alone when he needs to rest. You must also consider how the younger dog will react, once the older dog eventually comes to the end of his life – perhaps you should think about getting another companion fairly soon, so that the younger dog is not lonely?

When to Say Goodbye
During the course of writing this book, I had to make the awful decision to have a beloved dog put to sleep, to save her any further suffering. It is something I have had to face many times during my dog-owning years, and it never gets any easier. It is also something that perhaps you don't want to think about, just as you are embarking upon your first experience of owning a dog. It is, however, an inevitable fact of life that, unless your dog dies naturally, at some stage you, as a caring, responsible owner, are going to have to make the decision to end the dog's life.

There is an expression that many dog owners use when deciding when the time should come. It is 'Quality of Life' – and here I am talking about the dog's life, not the human's. In other words, is the dog still enjoying the important things in life – walking, eating and being cuddled – without pain or embarrassment at being unable to do the things he once could? It may sound strange to imply that a dog can feel embarrassment, but I know that dogs do feel a lack of dignity if, for example, they can no longer climb the stairs, of if they have a house-training accident indoors.

The decision to have a dog put to sleep should be based on the dog's ability to cope with the processes of ageing, rather than *your inability* to cope! Just because he may be a bit smelly, or not so much fun to play with, or may soil the carpet occasionally, this is not a good enough reason to end his life. Sadly, that is the premise on which some people decide to have their dog put to sleep – perhaps we should be grateful that they are not in charge of the NHS!

With my own beautiful 'Miggi', a Bernese Mountain Dog of ten and a half years, the decision was made with complete clarity when it was apparent that, after slowly declining for the previous year, her body had finally given up on her. She had a chronic liver condition which was being managed well with medication, and her arthritic joints were being kept mobile, again with medication. Came the day when she did not want to get up for breakfast, could not even give me a wag of her tail, and I knew immediately that she had had enough. It may well be that we could have asked the vet to give her treatment that may have prolonged her life for a week or two, and which may have helped my husband and me by putting off the inevitable, but it certainly would not have done Miggi any favours. Fortunately, we have a superb vet who came to the house so quickly, and Miggi left this life with dignity, in her own home with her 'humans' by her side.

If you have heard any horror stories of how a dog is put to sleep, please cast them from your mind. The vet will usually inject the dog with an overdose of barbiturate, which is a type of anaesthetic, and the dog literally 'goes to sleep'. It is done with dignity, sympathy and understanding, and the last act that you can do for your dog is to make sure that you are there, holding him, when his life finally ends.

15

Introducing a Second Dog Into the Home

Nowadays, many families are becoming multi-dog. They start with one, then get another as company for the first one and so on. Normally, second and subsequent dogs join the family without any problems, but there are things which you can do to aid the acceptance process.

Generally speaking, if you already have a male dog, it is better to choose a female as the second dog. There is less risk of fighting between male and female, whereas male dogs can be very territorial and resent another male dog intruding on their territory. Naturally, care must be taken with a male and female dog in the same household when the bitch comes into season, but having her spayed after the first season will resolve that problem. There *is* a slight possibility that once your male dog has a female dog for a companion, he may become a little possessive towards her, by showing aggression to other male dogs who approach his bitch.

Whichever sex you decide upon, try and arrange for their first meeting to be on neutral territory, in case the first dog should show any territorial aggression towards the newcomer. Obviously, if the new dog is a young puppy, you will have to bring the pup straight home, but make sure that the first dog's favourite and most loved member of the family is not the one who carries the puppy indoors. Usually, whatever sex the new puppy is, the original dog will make allowances, and will recognise it as a baby, who offers no threat to his position within the family.

Whether it's a puppy or an older dog, both dogs will

adjust more easily if you accept that between them, *they* will work out who is going to be boss dog over the other. Don't try and use human logic by assuming that the dog who was in the house first should be number one dog. It may turn out that way, but if it doesn't and you interfere and upset the natural order of things, you could end up with a very unpleasant situation. By watching their behaviour towards one another, you will quickly see which dog is showing signs of subservience. The underdog will possibly lie down when the other approaches and sniffs him. He may allow the other dog to take his food – here you *should* interfere, by feeding the two dogs separately, or you will end up with one very overweight dog! Boss dog will demonstrate his superiority by pushing the other out of the way when affection is in the offing. He will always try to be the first out of the door when going for walks and first into the car when going for a ride. He may well threaten the other dog verbally, to instil his dominance.

Don't try to treat the two dogs as equals – in their world equality does not exist, remember their basic instincts. Once the pecking order has been established, don't be tempted to compensate the underdog by cuddling him more than the boss dog, or feeding him an extra titbit. This will merely antagonise the boss dog, who will then punish his subordinate for what he considers to be liberty-taking and getting above his position.

Always allow boss dog to be first through the door, after you. Feed him first, welcome him first when you come in. You are not showing favouritism by doing this – you're simply accepting the natural order which both dogs recognise.

If you have an elderly dog and are bringing a young puppy into the household, you must obviously take care that the boisterous behaviour of the youngster does not harm the old dog. The youngster will obviously want to play and here you can shield the older dog a little, by getting on to the floor and playing with the pup yourself, to deflect unwanted attention away from the older one. Having said that, don't interfere when the older dog tells the puppy off. He must be allowed to put the pup in his place, or the youngster could make the older dog's life a misery.

Very often, you find that bringing a young puppy into the household can revitalise the older dog, so don't worry too much, just be sensible.

Whilst on the subject of having second and subsequent dogs, please don't be tempted to get two puppies together, as this can have disastrous consequences. I have a friend who says that 'puppy plus puppy equals puppy squared' and it will certainly feel like that at times – two puppies together can wreak the havoc of four!

Firstly, the puppies will always relate to one another, before you, especially if they are litter brothers or sisters, as they will have been together since birth. Two puppies living together will form an attachment that is far more important to them than any human attachment. They will gang-up, as together they are a pack. Because they are a pack, they may become aggressive to other, single dogs.

If one is a chewer, he will influence the non-chewer, not the other way around. They will compete with one another at every opportunity. Walking on the lead will turn into a race, as will getting out of the front door, getting to their food, etc. If one is a barker, he will encourage the other to bark. Having two together will lead you to lump them together, rather than letting their individual characters emerge. When it comes to house-training, the slower of the two to become clean may influence the other into being unclean again.

I could cite many more examples of why having two puppies together could be a dreadful combination. If you feel that I am coming on strong on this subject, it is because many years ago I did exactly what I'm trying to deter you from doing. I obtained two dear little cross-bred puppies – I just couldn't separate them – and the ensuing round of catastrophes led me to joining a dog training club and getting hooked on dog training! I would add that both dogs lived to a grand age, but not before they had made a good job of trying to wreck each other, my home and my nerves! Since then, I have met many people who have made the same mistake and were pulling their hair out over the antics of their puppies. So, if it is your intention to go and get two puppies, please think again. Get one first, let him reach maturity, then go and get the second.

16

Some of the More Popular Breeds

The top three breeds in the UK are, in order, the Labrador, the German Shepherd (Alsatian) and the Cocker Spaniel. Others in the top ten list include the Golden Retriever, the West Highland White Terrier (Westie), the Cavalier King Charles Spaniel, the Boxer, the Rottweiller, the English Springer Spaniel, and the Staffordshire Bull Terrier (Staffie). As a dog trainer, I see many examples of these and the other more popular breeds, and as such I would probably try to talk most people out of owning any of them, simply because I see more of the ones who have problems! I see the results of either illogical treatment by the owners, or of the wrong choice made, or the outcome of people breeding dogs for money, and breeding from unsuitable stock, rather than to improve their particular breed.

Obviously, there are some lovely examples of all the different breed types – and crossbreeds. To help you perhaps finally make up your mind which dog to pick, I have asked some owners to relate their own experience of living with and owning some of the more popular breeds. I asked them to be honest, and give the negative side as well as the positive side to having their particular breed within their family. I have added my own comments after each 'testimonial'.

Bichon Frise
'I have two of these dogs – a two-year-old bitch called "Phoebe" and a nine-month-old puppy called "Fabs". I find them delightful little dogs; intelligent, full of fun

Fig. 31. Bichon Frise.

and good with children. Fabs is inclined to panic at unknown sights and sounds but Phoebe is much more placid and will investigate and bark at anything. They are good guard dogs, as they have a big bark for such a small dog – (they say 'Woof Woof', not 'Yap Yap') – and they have excellent hearing.

'Grooming is probably one of the biggest disadvantages and expenses of owning this breed. They need to be combed every day, which takes about fifteen minutes. They don't moult, but need to be clipped every six weeks at the grooming parlour. They also need to be bathed regularly, as they are all-white dogs and can get very dirty. My two have been taught properly to stand and be groomed and to be bathed, and so thoroughly enjoy the experience but, if you had a dog who did not enjoy it, I imagine it would make life very difficult!

'They are both rather faddy eaters, and eat slowly. They are not keen on proprietary brand dog foods, so I tend to give them fresh, home cooked meat or chicken, with potatoes, vegetables and gravy. They are fed twice a day, morning and evening.

'Training them to be obedient was relatively easy, as they enjoyed the titbits and fuss when they "got it right", although, like many dogs, they choose not to understand sometimes! House-training was not so easy, and the younger one still has the odd accident indoors. They enjoy the company of other dogs, irrespective of their size, and mix well with people. They also get on well with the family cat.

'They like going out for walks, but Fabs hates wind and rain and just won't walk in bad weather. Neither of them likes the car very much, but since getting a travelling cage, they are now no longer sick and can travel a couple of hundred miles.

'To sum up, I would say they are very loving dogs, and are devoted to the members of their family. They love to be cuddled, to sit on laps and to sleep on the bed, and overall are utterly charming companions.'

This owner has given a very honest account of living with her Bichons. She has worked hard on training, and has adopted a sensible attitude to having small dogs, not treating them like babies or toys. Because of the white fur, they are a fairly high maintenance dog, so you must find the time to bathe and groom them regularly, or have the money to pay a grooming parlour to do the job for you. The behavioural problems with small dogs are usually initiated by the owners, who sometimes forget that, whatever the size, he is still a DOG.

Border Collie

Fig. 32. Border Collie.

'The Border Collie is the workaholic of the dog world. Bred for generations to herd sheep in areas where it would be impossible to farm without a dog, where stamina and intelligence need to be matched with strength of character, this breed is now exported all over the world and is well-known for its working ability. The versatility of the collie is also demonstrated in the way he can turn his paw to a variety of other jobs such as Search and Rescue, as well as excelling in Obedience, Agility and Working Trials.

'To the layman it would then seem logical that such a talented breed would therefore make an ideal pet. However, the very virtues that help to make them the ideal working dog can result in just the opposite. Border Collies have insatiable curiosity and energy and need considerable exercise. Not just physical exercise either – many a misguided owner has tried to calm their dog down by giving them plenty of free running, only to have ended up with a super-fit hooligan instead! Living with a Collie is a little like having a hyper-active, gifted child – they need attention, problems to solve and a leader they can respect.

'It is true that Border Collies are intelligent and learn quickly. Over the generations they have been selected for this ability, as few shepherds have the time or resources to coach the slow starters. Much of the training that they receive serves to bring out natural instincts that are well-fixed in the breed. In a pet home these instincts can be aroused by quick movement, shadows, other animals, children and even cars. These can be seen in circling, fixations, chasing, nipping and other unwanted activities. Border Collies can learn undesirable behaviour as readily as they learn the things that we intend to teach them – they are masters at reading body language and have incredibly quick reactions.

'Many Border Collies end up being re-homed or put down through no fault of their own, because their owners, often well-meaning, have failed to appreciate what they are taking on. If you want to live with a

Border Collie, do your research carefully. Avoid buying at the farm gate, and find a litter that has been bred from a bitch with a sensible temperament. Start training early, find a good training class and be prepared to spend a considerable amount of time playing with and training your dog. Find out as much as you can about the breed so that you understand the instincts that drive your dog, and use them to your advantage. Remember that Collies often live to 15 years old or more, so the foundations that you build in puppyhood will be with you for many years to come.'

This owner has lived with and trained Border Collies for over thirty years, and her description of them is absolutely spot on. Unless you are committed to working your Border Collie, either in the obedience ring, working trials or agility, they are not suitable as just a 'pet' dog.

Boxer
'He arrived in my home aged eight weeks old, took one look at my big, gentle Irish Wolfhound of five years old, and barked at him. We of course laughed, but little did we realise then that the pattern was set – "Arnie" decided that his purpose in life was to entertain his

Fig. 33. Boxer.

human family at every opportunity, and to sort out any dog he didn't like the look of!

'As he grew, so did his boldness. In my opinion, the difference between an aggressive dog and a fighter is the size of their "victim". Arnie falls into the latter group – small dogs have nothing to fear from him and with puppies he is the perfect "uncle". However, bigger dogs are a different ball game. He has never bitten any dog (or human), but is the canine equivalent of a stroppy teenager out on a Saturday night looking for bother. Always bigger than him, the dogs which Arnie doesn't like are easy to spot, usually breeds which themselves have a reputation – Rottweilers, Dobermans, German Shepherd Dogs, Japanese Akitas – I have never been sure if he isn't just reliving World War Two single-pawed!

'Having learnt to live with this one albeit serious character blip, the pluses and pleasures connected with living with Arnie are immeasurable. He gives love, loyalty and devotion which is second to none. He is totally protective and committed. Anyone who visits the house for the first time is subjected to his scrutiny, when he will sit firmly at my feet, between me and the caller. However, my friends soon become his, especially little girls, and he has learnt the art of looking cute, resulting in people almost falling over themselves to give him a titbit. Even now, at twelve years old, he still has the "Ahhh" factor.

'If other dogs are not on Arnie's list of loves (apart from his special canine friends) cats can do no wrong in his eyes – and not just his own house cat, who he happily allows to share his bed. Any of the neighbourhood cats are welcomed into our house and garden by Arnie, where they can stay as long as they like.

'Most Boxers have strong personalities and Arnie is no exception – he has a very strong character and can sometimes be wilful. At training classes he quickly became the class clown. Coming back to me, to be rewarded by a titbit and a cuddle, was nowhere near as rewarding as visiting all the other owners first; perhaps popping his head around the kitchen door to say hello to anyone making tea was much more fun.

'Arnie has had to learn to adapt to many changes within the household. As a younger dog, he had the company of my children. Now, with them all having flown the nest, it is just me and him, but he seems perfectly happy, welcoming them home when they visit, but resigned and accepting that they will leave again. The plus side is that Arnie and I have enjoyed many holidays together, staying in dog friendly guest houses and hotels all over England. All in all, he seems very content to be with me, and I am just so grateful to have the opportunity of sharing my life, my settee and occasionally (when he gets fed up with his own) the end of my bed, with a Boxer.'

As this lady's experiences prove, Boxers are real characters and vie for the title of clown of the dog world. I have encountered some truly lovely boxers, but also a fair proportion of those I have met have been dog aggressive, so choose the temperament very carefully if this is the breed for you. Not for the faint hearted, nor for the easily embarrassed, and certainly not for the shrinking violets.

Cavalier King Charles Spaniel
'Emma', 'Annie' and 'Chloe'
'In 1983, after ten "dogless" and unrestricted years with regards to holidays, etc., my husband and I decided that we would love to have a dog once more. Our last dog had been a yellow Labrador but, as we were now not quite so young and fit, we thought it might be better to have a smaller dog, that wouldn't need quite so much exercise. After searching through several books on different breeds, we decided that we would like a CKC Spaniel, and that we preferred the black and tan, rather than the tri-coloured. We then visited some dog shows and spoke to the exhibitors, asking if they could recommend a good breeder and eventually found a lady who had just bred a litter of puppies.

217

We decided to have a bitch this time, as we had been told that bitches tended to be gentler and more affectionate than dogs, and this lady happened to have a bitch left. We saw the puppies at aged four weeks and they were gorgeous! While the rest of the litter played around the room, "our" little one just wanted to be cuddled, which we rather liked. She was nine weeks old when we collected her and we named her "Emma". She was the easiest puppy imaginable – she had toys of her own and never attempted to chew anything else. She was rather difficult to house-train, but this was achieved eventually, with a lot of patience on our part. As an adult dog, she was one of the most affectionate dogs towards people, although she was always timid with other dogs. She lived to over 14 years of age – quite a long time for this breed – and we were devastated when she died.

'My husband was not keen on having another dog for a while, but after five weeks I was nearly climbing the walls! He was "persuaded" to have another and we soon found "Annie". She was already four months old, as her breeder had been going to keep her for showing, but thought her teeth were not coming through quite right and therefore decided to sell her (in fact, her teeth turned out perfectly!). What a shock this pup turned out to be. For one thing, we had forgotten what it was like to have a puppy and, for another, Annie was a law unto herself! She thought she was the boss and she was also a hunter. When out on walks, she would disappear into the nearest bushes and often we wouldn't see her for about the next twenty minutes – which was very alarming to say the least. In the end, in desperation we contacted a dog behaviourist (yes, it was Jackie), who taught us how to make Annie realise that we were the bosses, not her! We also took her to training classes, where she proved to be extremely intelligent, and eventually we had the kind of dog we wanted – one who would actually walk with us, and since then she has been an absolutely wonderful companion – although the sight of a rabbit, squirrel or deer, etc., does immediately make her remember her old instincts and give chase, but she soon returns.

'When Annie was about two years old, we felt she was getting "old before her time". She tended to plod along and not to play very much, so we decided to get another dog to keep her company and hopefully re-awaken her spirit. Along came "Chloe", aged seven weeks, and the two dogs got on together right from the beginning. Chloe is nowhere near as intelligent as Annie, but is a sweet little girl, very, very affectionate and exceptionally good-tempered. The two of them are wonderful companions and adore each other. Chloe is, however, like Emma before her, rather nervous of other dogs.

We do not think we would ever have any other breed now. Cavaliers are wonderfully good-natured and easy to look after, beautiful and affectionate and we would recommend them to anyone.'

Knowing these dogs, I can't disagree with one word! Annie and Chloe are absolute sweeties. My husband and I have decided that when the time comes to admit that we can't cope with big dogs in the house, we are definitely going to have Cavaliers!

Cocker Spaniel – Two Different Owners' Viewpoints
'Toffee'
'I wanted a dog who would get on with my grandchildren, who are always visiting the house. I liked the look of the Cocker Spaniel but was worried about their reputation for being a bit snappy. I eventually found a breeder who was breeding from carefully chosen stock, with the specific aim of improving temperament, and as a result I chose Toffee, named after the colour of his coat.

'As a puppy, Toffee wasn't that lively; in fact the only game he really enjoyed was "chase" – first stealing a sock or a duster, and then getting the children to chase him around the house. He was not an easy puppy to

Fig. 34. Cocker Spaniel.

train, toilet training in particular was an arduous business! Even now, at eight years old, when I am displeased with him he simply wags his tail. Toffee's guiding force is food – he once stole the Christmas turkey – and on walks he will scavenge anything dead. He is quite lazy, and during the daytime is happiest sleeping on the sofa in the sunshine. He tolerates other dogs, but prefers their owners, knowing that his gentle eyes and sweet face will usually win him a biscuit! He is a bit of an enigma, but we love him very much.'

'Daisy'
'The first few years living with Daisy posed the problem of how to meet her high energy demands without overexciting her – not easy when you have children around. Even now, at seven years old, visiting new places with Daisy can be very demanding. She has always been very vocal, barking at unfamiliar sounds or when wanting attention.

'She appears content to be left alone in her own home, but she panics if left in anyone else's house and will try to dig her way out. Her hunting instinct is very strong and I need to be one step ahead of her or she is liable to take off after the smell of deer, pheasant or cat!

'Grooming can be hard unless she is regularly clipped, otherwise her coat mats, collecting thorns and grass seeds, etc. Temperamentally, she adores people, and is fairly submissive with other dogs.'

In recent years, Cocker Spaniels have had a bit of a reputation for being aggressive. I think that breeders are addressing the problem now, and those which have attended my training club over the past couple of years have certainly not been too problematical. I would be doubtful about introducing them to very young children, however, and perhaps Cockers are not the best choice for first-time owners.

Crossbreeds

'I have found that one of the main differences between owning pedigree dogs and crossbred dogs is to my bank balance! All my dogs have been individual and special, no matter what their parentage or lineage, but, on the whole, I have found that the crossbreeds have been much hardier and more intelligent, although I have to say that I have found no difference in the loyalty and love given.

' "Willie", the current oldest of my dogs, is a Staffordshire Bull Terrier-Whippet cross, and both breeds are very evident in his character and appearance. He is loyal, fast, strong and can be very protective at times. Due to ill treatment in his previous home, he is unable to be left alone and is very sensitive. He can shown signs of nervousness – possibly from the Whippet side of his parentage, and can occasionally be belligerent. In spite of being badly treated before he came to me, he loves people totally once he really gets to know them, and is beside himself with joy when my son is around.

' "Woody", also a rescued dog, is a Labrador-Greyhound cross. He has a deep-barrelled chest, and has the appearance of a Labrador, but more finely built. He is extremely sociable, lovable and unaware of his size when galloping up to greet people. He was born with a bone condition called Metaphysical Osteopathy (the result of crossing a chunky Labrador with the long-legged, deep-chested Greyhound), which affects his back legs. This causes him to be very prone to arthritis and as a result he does not have a great deal of stamina, making him the exception to the rule when it comes to crossbreeds being stronger and healthier than pedigrees. He has the sweetest nature and loves everyone, especially children.

' "Elbie", yet another rescued dog, is a Chihuahua-Yorkshire Terrier cross. She looks more like a Yorkshire Terrier, but has the big eyes and feathered ears of the Chihuahua. She is fearless, friendly and is the best house dog of the three. She adores children and has never growled or curled her lip at anyone. She plays hard with the two bigger dogs and puts them in their place when necessary. She has all the ratting traits of the Yorkie and will "kill" socks and towels by shaking them hard, as she would a rat to break its neck. She will take as much or as little exercise as is offered, and is at her happiest when sitting on someone's lap.'

It is obviously impossible to generalise about cross-breeds, simply because the variety is so huge and probably inexhaustible. This lady has three totally different types of dog, yet all are classed as crossbreeds. I have also owned crossbreeds – two Collie-Labrador crosses – and, although litter brothers, they were very different in temperament, as one took on more of the Collie character, whilst the other was typically Labrador. The definite plus was that they lived to a good age – 13 years and 16 years respectively.

Dalmatian
'We live with two Dalmatians. "Rusper" is nine years old and has been with us since he was eight weeks old. He is very docile and likes a quiet life. He is obedient when out unless he spies anything that may be edible, at which point he becomes completely impervious to all commands! He was well-socialised as a puppy and is

Fig. 35. Dalmatian.

happy to meet any other dogs. On the whole he is very placid but extremely lovable and is adored by all the family.

' "Penny" is something else! A very typical Dalmatian, active and alert at all times. We acquired her from Dalmatian Rescue when she was two years old, and we have had her for four years. It was apparent that she had not been well-trained, and considered herself top dog in every respect. She fought with Rusper at first, and both my husband and I were bitten when we tried to stop the fights. I took her to training classes, which have helped her to become more sociable, but we still have to take care when meeting dogs she doesn't know – in particular she seems to hate Jack Russell Terriers. She is very good with adults, but I would not trust her with children and she has tried to bite our grandchildren when they are noisy or rushing about, so we supervise any interaction very carefully.

'One of the problems in the breed is deafness, which is genetic. Make sure that the breeder you are considering buying from is breeding from dogs which have been tested, to ensure that they do not produce deaf puppies. Fortunately, neither of our dogs has a hearing problem (except when it suits them!).

'Dalmatians are extremely adept at stealing food – nothing is safe that is even remotely edible. Our two have stolen chocolate in vast quantities (which is extremely bad for dogs), a kilo bag of cat biscuits, bait from fishermen and even complete fish. Fortunately, they have managed to devour all of this, and more, without so far having any ill effects. Whenever Dalmatian owners meet, we swap stories of whose dog has managed the most spectacular theft!

'I would not recommend that a first-time dog owner takes on a Dalmatian, even though I love the breed and would never have any other. They are certainly not the easiest of dogs to train, they need plenty of exercise (at least two good walks a day, and in *all* weathers) and, if not exercised enough, will become overweight, even more restless indoors and probably destructive too.'

This is a 'feet on the ground' opinion of living with these dogs. They have become very popular once again, due to certain recent films, and if you are considering getting one, please look beyond their pretty appearance. I see quite a few Dalmatians at my classes, and it is rare to find a dog who is aggressive towards people, although some of the males can be a bit pushy with other dogs.

German Shepherd Dog (GSD or Alsatian) – Two Different Owners' Viewpoints
'Foley'
'You will need a great deal of time, patience and energy to reap the positive benefits of owning a GSD. If you get it right, the loyalty and affection they give to their owner is second to none.

'I would not recommend them if you have children, even though I have a child. I have had to teach my son to respect my dog and to understand that Foley needs his own space sometimes, within the family. Of course, I have also had to train Foley to respect my son, but I have never left them alone unsupervised, and, although Foley adores children, I have to be very observant when

Fig. 36. German Shepherd.

my son has his friends round, as children can quite innocently provoke dogs.

'German Shepherds need a great deal of mental stimulation as well as physical exercise, although running free should be limited until the dog is around a year old. My own dog is long-coated, and needs brushing daily to prevent the coat from getting matted, but even the short-coated types need grooming at least a couple of times a week.

'Some of my visitors are frightened of Foley, even though he is very well-trained, and that is something to be taken into account when thinking of buying a GSD.'

'Sadie', 'Megan', 'Brodie', 'Skye' and 'Annie'
'Having owned German Shepherds for twenty-two years, I believe that the breed is unsurpassed for showing loyalty and dedication. However, you yourself have to be the right temperament to live with such a spirited and alert breed. They thrive on physical and mental stimulation, love human interaction and need to feel part of the family; of course, knowing their place within that family is vital.

'If you really want a GSD, seek advice from other

owners, try and spend some time with their dogs and ask lots of questions so that you can get a "feel" for what it is really like to own one of these beautiful dogs. Go and see several breeders before you finally make your choice. Make sure that both the dam and sire of the puppy you choose are free from any possible hereditary conditions such as epilepsy and hip dysplasia.

'I owned my first dog before my children were born, and introducing them requires a great deal of care and common sense. The dog needs to know where he stands within the family and it is important that he does not feel rejected when a baby comes along. As my sons grew, the bond between them and the first and subsequent new canine additions developed, as did mutual respect. My boys were never allowed to tease or torment the dogs – young children cannot understand that dogs have feelings and can have an "off" day. I never allowed boisterous or noisy interaction between the children and the dogs – it is far too easy for accidents to occur.

'I have found GSDs to be very biddable with training, provided that you are logical and kind – harsh training will simply provoke the dog into acting defensively. Exercise was limited until my dogs were about a year old, and they were not allowed to run up or down stairs, as this can damage young growing bones. The GSD wants to learn – getting involved in obedience and agility provides them with physical and mental exercise, plus it is a great way to meet other like-minded owners.

'The breed does have a reputation for being "stand-offish" with strangers and other dogs. I have not experienced this myself, as I have always socialised my puppies thoroughly, taking them with me to meet my children from school, and actively involving them in our family life. All my dogs, past and present, have given my family enormous pleasure, and for me they are *the* most impressive breed.'

Both of these owners have painted a very accurate picture of GSDs. Often, these dogs are obtained for the wrong reasons, maybe as a guard dog or simply because they are impressive to look at and as such some people like the reaction they provoke. GSDs can be quite vocal, and often appear nervous of people or situations of which they are unsure. Unless you're really sure about what you're taking on, perhaps this is not the ideal dog for first-time ownership.

Golden Retriever – Three Different Owners' Viewpoints
'Jenna'
'I chose a bitch, as I had heard that the dogs could be fairly stubborn. Jenna was slow to mature, and stayed young and fun-loving for a long time. She is a bit scatty at times, but was easily trained and is trustworthy with children and gentle with all people and dogs. I have met other Retrievers who were not so gentle or good-tempered, and realise that picking the right breeder, plus going to training classes, is essential with this working breed.

'She loves getting wet and her coat, being long and feathery, requires a fair bit of attention afterwards, with brushing and drying.'

Fig. 37. Golden Retriever.

'George'

'George is our much loved 15-year-old Golden Retriever. He has been a pleasure to live with ever since he moved in with us. As a puppy he did all the usual chewing, etc., but if you leave things lying around, you have to expect that sort of thing.

'He has always had a wonderful and gentle temperament. He was easy to train, simply wanting to please, and loves children, adults and other dogs. If members of "his" family are in different rooms in the house, he will wander back and forth between us, puffing and blowing, and is only really relaxed when we are all together again. George loves his walks, although now he is elderly can only manage a short distance. He travels very well in the car and behaves well even on long distances. Any family would feel especially blessed to have had a Golden Retriever like our George.'

Since this was written, George became very frail and was subsequently put to sleep, to save him any suffering. I knew George, and agree with everything his owners have said about him – he was an absolute poppet and a pleasure to know.

'Monty' and 'Rommel'

'Once we had decided that our family should have a dog, we looked at the size and character of several breeds before deciding on a Golden Retriever. We wanted a dog that would be large enough to enjoy energetic walks, but would still fit into the confines of an urban semi. Temperamentally, the dog would have to be good with children, with an affectionate and trustworthy nature. We also wanted a dog who would not bring forth negative responses from neighbours or people in public areas. Finally, we wanted, where possible, to get a breed that did not have serious health or genetic defects. Golden Retrievers are known to have a predisposition towards hip problems, but overall we decided that this was the right breed for us.

'When we had found a suitable breeder, we were

invited to attend for an interview! The lady was extremely charming, but made it very clear that we had to prove that we would be suitable owners for one of her puppies. This required two extensive visits, before finally Monty was chosen and eventually came to live with us.

'He was an enthusiastic chewer, eating carpets, curtains and chair legs. A puppy cage (indoor kennel) proved an essential accessory, although at first we were very reluctant to use one, but the breeder strongly advised it and we were extremely grateful for such sound advice. Monty loved his den, and chewing and housetraining were then much easier to control, with Monty becoming clean indoors within two to three months.

'One of the biggest problems we have encountered, both with Monty and now with our new goldie puppy Rommel, is their enthusiasm for gardening! There is nothing they enjoy more than digging up the lawn (there is now none left), uprooting all the shrubs and flowers from the flower beds, hanging by their mouths from branches of small bushes and trees, and generally creating total garden chaos! I have to admit that, as we are not committed gardeners, the sight of them playing and having such obvious fun is more than adequate compensation for the total (but hopefully temporary) destruction of our garden.

'As an indication of how two dogs of the same breed can differ, when it comes to food, Monty is a slow eater and tends to become bored with the same food after a while. Rommel, on the other hand, never shows any reluctance and will eat what we put in front of him.

'Indoors, our dogs like to lie across the middle of the hall, causing quite a sizable obstruction. They have high energy levels, jumping and running about, and when their humans are sitting down they can expect to be sat on, nuzzled, hit in the face with a feathery, wagging tail, or trodden on. Being long-haired dogs, they seem constantly to shed vast quantities of hair, and, even with regular grooming of dogs and regular vacuuming of carpets, there is still dog hair to be found. They also "slobber", which causes unsightly stains on clothing!

'Outside, both dogs are extremely sociable, and a joy to take for a walk – the true pleasure of dog ownership for our family. We can take them anywhere, and have made many new friends as a result. The perceived image we had of Golden Retrievers was that of a loyal, loving, boisterous and friendly dog – we have certainly not been disappointed with either of our two, and they have certainly lived up to that reputation.

'We have been very fortunate both in our choice of breeder and our choice of dogs, and realise that there are bad examples of our breed too, but our experience has been such a good one that we would recommend Golden Retrievers for a family, particularly if they like walking, but do not enjoy gardening!'

Three lovely accounts of this very popular breed. All of these owners have made a point of training their dogs, so that the lovely nature of the breed has taken precedence. Untrained, they can be a bit pushy sometimes, but I have rarely come across a 'people aggressive' goldie – some of the males I have encountered have been a bit stroppy with other male dogs, but this is usually because of incorrect training, especially during puppyhood.

Great Dane

'Great Danes are lovable great hunks that will do their best to eat you out of house and home. They do not need as much exercise as some people think, as they have short bursts of energy and generally are content to plod around after you. In my experience their veterinary bills are proportionate to their size! They also have a short life span – anything over seven years is a bonus, which may not be ideal for a family dog, with the ensuing heartbreak that losing them relatively early brings. They are generally very loving and gentle, but obviously, because of their size, the home has to be adapted accordingly – no low tables with ornaments for a start! You also need to consider how your children's

Fig. 38. Great Dane.

friends will feel being confronted with a dog who may be bigger than them.'

Again, another very honest account of this particular breed. Perhaps for a family the high maintenance and short life span of a Great Dane is not ideal, plus being so large, interaction between the dog and the children will not be easy. I have encountered several Great Danes, and they have all been very gentle, in spite of their size.

Irish Setter (also known as Red Setter)
'I have owned Irish Setters for 25 years, and for me they are the ideal family dog. In all my years of living with this breed, I have only come across one dog with a suspect temperament, and this was with other dogs, not people.

'Many people think that Irish Setters are stupid, and that you can never get them back once you let them off the lead. This has not been my experience. If they appear to be scatty, this is due to lack of training. When taught correctly, with kind methods, you will have a fun-loving and intelligent companion for the duration of the dog's life. The average lifespan is between 10 and

Fig. 39. Irish Setter.

15 years, and they are slow to mature, not really being "grown up" until about seven years old.

'There are four types of setter. The Irish is red in colour, sometimes with a dash of white on the chest. The Red and White Setter is mainly white with splashes of red. The Gordon Setter – the largest of all setters – is black and tan. Finally, the English Setter, which can be orange (brown) and white, blue (grey) and white, or tricoloured, which is white, red and brown.

'Within the Irish Setters, I have only ever had males, but for a first–time dog owner I would suggest a bitch – the males tend to be stronger, both physically and mentally. Of course, with a bitch you will have to cope with her coming into season. Spaying is the obvious answer, but bear in mind that sometimes a spayed bitch's coat may go a bit fluffy afterwards.

'The Irish Setter has a beautiful silky coat, which will need regular attention – at least twice weekly grooming sessions to prevent it becoming matted. As to exercise, you will find it hard to wear them out! Obviously, when they are puppies, and until they are about nine months old, exercise should be limited, so that they don't damage their growing bones.

'Some Irish Setters can be fairly fussy eaters, so make sure that you get feeding advice and a diet sheet from the breeder. You should also check that, before both the dam and sire were bred from, they were both tested for the known defects within the breed, which can be passed on to their offspring. Ask about the following:

1. Mouths – an Irish Setter should have a scissor bite, i.e. the top set of teeth should fit cleanly and closely over the bottom set.
2. Eyes – Progressive Retinal Atrophy (PRA) was present in the breed a few years ago. It has now been virtually eradicated due to careful breeding, but make sure that the parents of the puppy are certified clear.
3. Canine Leucocyte Adhesion Deficiency (CLAD) is a comparatively recent problem which has affected some Irish Setters. It is an inherited immunodeficiency condition, causing various severe recurrent infections in the young dog, which respond poorly to antibiotics. The young dog gets progressively weaker, usually leading to euthanasia before the dog is six months old. The mutation associated with the severe form of CLAD has recently been identified and a DNA-based test for carrier detection is now available.
4. Irish Setters, being fairly large dogs, are also at risk from Gastric Dilation, so the necessary precautions should be taken when feeding your dog. (See Chapter 12, page 196.)

'Provided you take every precaution when choosing a breeder, your puppy should come to you in glowing health. Once you are the proud owner of this truly lovely breed, you will be addicted for life. They have beauty, intelligence and an enormous capacity for getting the very best out of life.'

A very knowledgeable account from this owner, who clearly knows her breed. I have personally never met a bad-tempered Setter, but they are not a breed for those who like a quiet, sedentary life!

233

Labrador – Two Owners' Viewpoints

'Kelly' and 'Poppy'

'Having had two, I would best describe them as being a bit like a bull in a china shop. Finesse does not spring to mind! Kelly was my first, followed later by Poppy, both Yellow Labradors. They were reasonably easy to train, but I have only ever had bitches, and talking to owners of male Labradors I have learned that the boys can be more difficult. They need lots of interesting exercise – a walk around a town park is not enough, and generally they are sociable with both people and other dogs, but will retaliate if another dog pushes them too far. Training needs to be kept interesting, or they quickly get bored. Coat care is easy – being short-coated a good brushing a couple of times a week is sufficient.'

'Cassie' and 'Stanley'

'When we decided to have Cassie and Stanley, brother and sister Black Labradors, we did not know that having two puppies together was not a very good idea! The first twelve months were quite difficult, mainly because we were never sure who had done what! Cassie is more obedient – she likes to play with a ball during

Fig. 40. Labrador.

234

our walks. Stanley is more difficult, as he can't resist going to see all of the other dogs, even if they are a long way away. Now he is older we don't panic so much, as he will now come back to us once he has said his "hello's".

'They are big, solid dogs, and tend to walk through things rather than around them. They have both knocked us over when playing and not looking where they were going. This boisterous behaviour can be a bit of a worry if there are young children around, although they are completely non-aggressive and love children and adults alike.

'They need loads of exercise and even after a long walk will still career around the house for a while before they crash out for a couple of hours. They love travelling in the car, and we hardly know they're there, as they are so good. The pleasure and entertainment they give us outweighs the problems, but I would certainly not recommend getting two puppies together, and will not do it again.'

As Labradors are currently the number one breed in the UK, it is understandable that I have seen more of them than any other breed. They are not as trainable for the pet home as the Golden Retriever, and the males especially can sometimes be difficult. They come in three colours: yellow, black and chocolate. They are extremely energetic dogs, especially as puppies, and need early training to channel their energies into things which you like them doing, rather than things you don't like!

Springer Spaniel – English
'What with working full-time, and then having a baby, I was dogless for several years. As soon as our daughter was old enough, and I then started working from home, I persuaded my husband that the time was right for us to have a dog. We looked at several breeds, from Beagles to Flat Coated Retrievers and at last agreed on the English Springer Spaniel. (As a child we had a Welsh Springer, so I knew a little about this boisterous breed!)

'We located a breeder, went to see the litter and fell head over heels in love with them all. The tiniest and shyest of them all swaggered towards my daughter, and as she bent down to him, he cowered! This was our destiny – after all, who would want a nervous Springer for a gun dog? Not necessarily the best reasons for choosing a particular puppy, but we were hooked – at least being nervous he would want to stay with us, rather than taking himself off for a walk.

' "Jerry Springer" became a dog that wanted to be with us everywhere, and his nervousness slowly waned, but he always wanted to be close to us. Eventually, we decided to add another Springer to our family and contacted English Springer Welfare. I filled in the form, stating young bitch, liver and white, working stock. There are vast numbers of Springers in rescue centres in the UK – mainly due to people getting them without realising what an active breed they are. We assumed we would have to wait several months – in fact within three weeks of completing our form, we were offered a bitch aged 13½ weeks, and asked whether we could collect her within the next two days! We were now a two Springer family!

' "Millie" came with a satchel full of problems, but we have ironed most of them out and she is now a loving, obedient dog. She takes part in plenty of mental activity, along with loads of physical exercise and plenty of banter and jaw wrestling with Jerry. As for Jerry, he takes part in all of the above, but he is the one with 100 per cent character – he's the one who brings our slippers to us with a glint in his eye; he's the one who sneaks onto our bed when we're out; he's the one who insists he's never heard the name Jerry at training classes and he's the one who knows exactly which buttons to press when he wants something! He is also very sensitive, extremely affectionate and excellent with children. To generalise about "our" breed, I would say that they are loyal, loving, beautiful, willing, challenging, energetic, fun, intelligent, friendly, working, useful dogs. They must not be left on their own for long periods of time, so not a breed to have if you are out at work all day – in fact, what dog is! Being a working dog, they can become very depressed, withdrawn and destructive, if left alone for long. They don't ask for too much – just lots of things to occupy their brains, lots of love and attention and PLENTY of exercise (not just around the park), but long and interesting walks to satisfy their curious instinct. A change of walk at least every other day, preferably through woods, up hill and down dale, including some "water" activity, hopefully meeting other dogs and also finding some birds to "get up"!

'Some of the activities you can entertain Springers with include:

1. **Basic Obedience** mainly focusing on respect which must be gained quickly, as Springers can become dominant and stubborn.
2. **Competitive Obedience** – yes, Springers can be trained to Border Collie standard in the ring.
3. **Gun Dog Work /Field Trials** – even if you are not going to go on a shoot, this can be fun and rewarding for your dog. Be careful though, as some gun dog trainers can be harsh, so be sure you find one with gentle training methods.
4. **Agility** – Springers just adore this sport.
5. **Fly ball** – fantastic fun and creates great teamwork, but your Springer must retrieve well first.
6. **Tracking** – brilliant, brain occupying work for a Springer.
7. **At Home** – hide an object and get your dog to find it – it will keep him occupied for quite a while!
8. **Tricks** – being so eager to please, your dog will enjoy being taught a number of tricks.

'So, life with our Springers is just about perfect – in fact, the only thing better than having two Springers would be more of the same!

Anything I added about this breed would be superfluous – this knowledgeable owner has said it all!

Springer Spaniel – Welsh

'Having had Welsh Springers for many years, my advice is don't get one if you're easily embarrassed or very house-proud! At training classes, you will be the owner with the reddest face as your dog will think of at least three other things he'd rather do than the thing you are asking of him. He will not look at you adoringly whilst walking to heel, as he will be too busy sniffing the floor or the dog nearest to him. On walks he will jump into all available muddy water – the smellier the better! He will go off hunting rabbits and pheasants, and will track them for miles. He will need lots of exercise – he was bred to work all day.

'At home, he will follow you and be at your side whenever possible, so must be trained carefully to accept that sometimes he must remain in one room whilst you are in another, otherwise he will develop separation anxiety. If you are working full-time you should not contemplate getting a Welsh Springer – they are such a sociable breed and thrive on human company. He will need to have his feet and ears trimmed regularly, so you will need to learn how to do this, or take him to a grooming parlour.

'A Welsh Springer will adore you, greet you with wild enthusiasm, won't go looking for trouble from other

Fig. 41. Welsh Springer Spaniel.

dogs, but will be courageous if provoked. If you're lucky he will live to about twelve years old, starting to slow down at about eight years old. He will love everyone and will be a happy, outgoing character.'

A lovely working breed, which is fairly adaptable to living within a family, provided they are not left to their own devices for long periods of time. This owner knows her breed and her description of their character is extremely accurate. The Welsh Springer is a very energetic and amusing dog and will make a good family pet, provided they are properly trained and given sufficient exercise.

West Highland White (Westie)

'I chose a Westie because of the way they look and because of their size. Having now owned one for nearly two years, I wouldn't change "Sophie" for anything, but if I was considering having a second dog, I wouldn't have another Westie – I think one is more than enough for any family!

'Her good points ... Sophie learnt quickly, which surprised me as I was apprehensive at first, with her being a terrier I had heard how difficult they can be. She really enjoyed the classes and loved the socialising with the other puppies. She will now sit, lie down and come

Fig. 42. West Highland White.

239

when called, and will sit and wait nicely whilst I attach her lead. Staying when told is not one of her strong points, but she can do it, and in general is as obedient as I need her to be. She loves the company of other dogs, especially if they are bigger than her. She is very enthusiastic about going for a walk – I take her out for one on-the-lead walk a day, plus she has about half an hour running in the park daily. She still tries to pull on the lead, but is slowly getting better!

'Sophie is brushed every day – her coat is quite thick and she has not been clipped, so her coat can get matted if not looked after. She also has a bath at least every six weeks. Fortunately, she enjoys both these activities. Westies are particularly prone to flea allergies, so I have to ensure that flea prevention treatment is regularly applied.

'Her not so good points . . . As far as Sophie is concerned, cats are for chasing – she doesn't hurt them, but just seems to enjoy the chase. If they stop running, so does she. She is very jealous of our cats, and does not like it when one of them is on my lap – she will continually try to get my attention until eventually the cat goes away. I would not trust her with any small animals such as guinea pigs, hamsters or rabbits, as sadly she did kill our hamster.

'Sophie considers that the garden is solely there for her to excavate, and the lawn is now covered with masses of holes. She also barks at every single noise when she is outside, and also barks a fair bit indoors too – noises on the TV will start her off. However, when we visit friends or family, she does not bark in their houses or gardens.

'I have four children, the oldest being 13 years and the youngest four years. I do not think that Westies are particularly good with children, and would not recommend them with children under ten years old. Sophie has snapped at my two youngest children and will grumble at them if they come near me when she is beside me. She is also very possessive with food, whether it is hers or food left on the table, and will sit beside it and growl at the cats or the children if they go near it. The only person she does not growl at in the family is me, whom she seems to idolise, following me everywhere I go.

'Whether some of these bad points are to do with her breeding, or whether it is simply that I did not understand the breed enough, I'm not sure. I would not want to be without her, but she is certainly not the easiest dog to live with.'

This is a real 'warts and all' account of living with this tough little dog. They are now very popular, but you must be aware that they like to dominate and need logical and early training to get the best out of them. Coat care can be demanding, and their activity ratio is not in proportion to their size!

Yorkshire Terrier
' "Barney" was my first pet and for a year it was just him, until two more dogs and three cats joined the family. Even as a small puppy he was fearless and is completely undaunted by larger dogs. He is good-natured, patient, obedient and rarely growls. He does bark at other dogs when out for walks, rushing up to them in a bossy manner and telling them in no uncertain terms to mind their Ps and Qs, but is not aggressive

Fig. 43. Yorkshire Terrier.

and soon makes friends with canines and humans alike.

'He has plenty of energy and copes very well with long walks. He has an obsession with chasing balls, and once he has retrieved a ball will do everything in his power to hang on to it. My sons have named him "Sniper" because of his deadly accuracy when snatching a ball from their hands.

'He has a long coat which if kept unclipped requires a huge amount of grooming, so I have Barney regularly clipped, as I do not want to show him.

'All in all he is a loyal and loving pet, and holds a very special place in my heart.'

This lady has treated her dog as a dog, not as a toy, and so has extracted the very best out of him. Too often, these tiny dogs are treated as ornaments, and end up pampered and spoilt. Because of their size, they could be at risk if you have clumsy children around, and they do not take well to being mauled about.

Summing Up

I hope that reading these personal experiences of some of the breeds has helped you. I am sure that for every positive comment made about a particular breed, someone else would make a negative one, and vice versa. Choosing the right breeder, and then raising the puppy in a logical (for the dog) way is vital.

There is a huge variety of dogs to choose from, and the following lists include most of the better known breeds, under their various groups. Obviously to write about each of them individually would take at least another half dozen books, so when you choose the breed you like the sound of, start doing your homework and find out everything you can.

Whether you choose a pedigree or crossbreed, I hope you find that this book has helped with that initial decision, and will continue to help throughout your dog owning life.

17

Breed Lists

Sporting Breeds
Hounds – Dogs bred for hunting by trailing or by sight.
Basenji
Basset Hound
Beagle
Bloodhound
Borzoi
Dachshund – Long-haired, Miniature Long-haired, Smooth-haired, Wire-haired, Miniature Wire-haired
Deerhound
Elkhound

Fig. 44. Bloodhound.

Finnish Spitz
Foxhound
Greyhound
Hamiltonstovare
Ibizan Hound
Irish Wolfhound
Otterhound
Pharaoh Hound
Rhodesian Ridgeback
Saluki
Whippet

Gundogs – Bred for either hunting, pointing, flushing out game or retrieving. Some of the breeds are multi-purpose, incorporating some or all of these traits.
Brittany Spaniel
English Setter
German Short-haired Pointer
German Wire-haired Pointer
Gordon Setter
Hungarian Vizla
Hungarian Wire-haired Vizla

Fig. 45. English Setter.

Irish Red and White Setter
Irish Setter
Italian Spinone
Large Munsterlander
Pointer
Retriever – Chesapeake Bay, Curly Coated, Flat Coated,
    Golden, Labrador
Spaniel – American Cocker, Cavalier King Charles,
    King Charles Spaniel, Clumber Spaniel, English
    Springer, Welsh Springer, English Cocker, Field, Irish
    Water, Sussex
Weimaraner

*Terriers – Dogs bred to assist mankind in various forms of
vermin control, some for digging out quarry, some for
following horses and then going to ground, digging out
foxes, badgers, martens, rats, etc.*
Airedale Terrier
Australian Terrier
Bedlington Terrier
Bull Terrier – Miniature, English, Staffordshire
Cairn Terrier
Dandie Dinmont Terrier
English Toy Terrier
Fox Terrier – Smooth, Wire-coated
Glen of Imaal Terrier
Irish Terrier
Jack Russell Terrier
Kerry Blue Terrier
Lakeland Terrier
Maltese Terrier
Manchester Terrier
Norfolk Terrier
Norwich Terrier
Parson Jack Russell Terrier
Scottish Terrier
Sealyham Terrier
Skye Terrier

Fig. 46. Jack Russell.

Soft-Coated Wheaten Terrier
Welsh Terrier
West Highland White Terrier
Yorkshire Terrier

Non-Sporting Breeds
Working Dogs – Bred to guard and protect either live-stock, property or people, and sometimes to attack where necessary. Some also used as drove dogs.
Alaskan Malamute
Bernese Mountain Dog
Bouvier des Flandres
Boxer
Bullmastiff
Doberman
Eskimo Dog
Giant Schnauzer
Great Dane
Hovawart
Leonburger
Mastiff
Neopolitan Mastiff
Newfoundland
Pinscher
Portuguese Water Dog
Rottweiler

Fig. 47. Doberman.

St. Bernard
Siberian Husky
Tibetan Mastiff

Pastoral
Dogs bred for herding and/or driving cattle and sheep.
Anatolian Shepherd Dog
Australian Cattle Dog
Bearded Collie
Belgian Shepherd Dog
Border Collie
Briard
Collie – Rough, Smooth
Estrela Mountain Dog
German Shepherd Dog (Alsatian)
Hungarian Kuvasz
Hungarian Puli
Komondor
Lancashire Heeler
Maremma Sheepdog
Norwegian Buhund
Old English Sheepdog
Polish Lowland Sheepdog

Fig. 48. Old English Sheepdog.

Pyrenean Mountain Dog
Samoyed
Shetland Sheepdog
Swedish Vallhund
Welsh Corgi – Cardigan, Pembroke

Utility
Dogs bred for a variety of different purposes, ranging from fighting bulls, hunting bear and deer, pulling sledges and carts, gundogs, and some simply for ornament.
Boston Terrier
Bulldog
Chow Chow
Dalmatian
French Bulldog
German Spitz
Japanese Akita
Japanese Shiba Inu
Japanese Spitz
Keeshond
Lhasa Apso
Miniature Schnauzer

Fig. 49. Bulldog.

Poodle – Standard, Miniature and Toy
Schipperke
Schnauzer
Shar Pei
Shih Tzu
Tibetan Spaniel
Tibetan Terrier

Toy Dogs
Some toy dogs have been included in the specific catego-
ries already listed, such as the Yorkshire Terrier, which is
included in the Terrier list. The following toy dogs do not
fit within the guidelines of the other groups, not having
been bred or used for a specific task. Some of them have
origins within other larger breeds and have been deliber-
ately bred smaller and smaller, until the size required was
arrived at, making them more suitable for being a pet or
lap dog.
Chihuahua – Long coat, Smooth coat
Chinese Crested
Griffon Bruxellois
Italian Greyhound
Japanese Chin
Miniature Pinscher
Papillon

Fig. 50. Chihuahua.

Pekingese
Pomeranian
Pug

Appendix – Useful Addresses

Barjo Engineering – Suppliers of indoor kennels, extension panels and car cages
Birchin Inhams Farm, Heathlands Road, Wokingham, Berkshire, RG40 3AP
Tel: 0118 9890240
Web: www.barjo.co.uk

Breed Rescues – Most veterinary surgeries have lists of individual breed rescues, or these can be obtained from the Kennel Club

The Company of Animals – Suppliers of remote control training collars
Ruxbury Farm, St Ann's Hill Road, Chertsey, Surrey, KT16 9NL
Tel: 01932 566696
E-Mail: office@companyofanimals.co.uk
Web: www.companyofanimals.co.uk

Dog Training Weekly – Weekly canine magazine
Print House, Parc Y Shwt, Fishguard, Dyfed, SA65 9AP

Dog World – Weekly canine magazine
Somerfield House, Wotton Road, Ashford, Kent, TN23 6LW

The Dogs Trust (Formerly known as The National Canine Defence League)
17 Wakley Street, London, EC1V 7RQ

Tel: 020 7837 0006
Web: www.dogstrust.org.uk

The Kennel Club
The Kennel Club, 1 Clarges Street, London, W1J 8AB
Tel: 0870 606 6750
E-Mail: info@the-kennel-club.org.uk
Web: www.the-kennel-club.org.uk

Natural Feeding – Suggested Reading
Raw Meaty Bones by Tom Lonsdale
Published by Rivetco P/L, PO Box 6096, Windsor
Delivery Centre, NSW 2756, Australia
E-mail: rivetco@rawmeatybones.com
Web: www.rawmeatybones.com

Useful Contact Point for new natural feeders:
http://groups.yahoo.com/group/rawfeeding/

Our Dogs – Weekly canine magazine
5 Oxford Road, Station Approach, Manchester, M60
1SX
Web: www.ourdogs.co.uk

Pet Travel Scheme (PETS)
Defra, Information Resource Centre, Lower Ground
Floor, Ergon House, c/o Nobel House, 17 Smith Square,
London SW1P 3JR
Web:www.defra.gov.uk/animalh/quarantine/pets/
procedures/owners.htm

**The Royal Society for the Prevention of Cruelty to
Animals (RSPCA)**
Enquiries Service, RSPCA, Wilberforce Way, Southwa-
ter, Horsham, West Sussex, RH13 9RS
General enquiries: 0870 3335 999
Emergency 24 hour hotline: 0870 5555 999
E-Mail: info@rspca.org.uk
Web: www.rspca.org.uk

Index

Adult dogs, 18–19, 204 *et seq.*

Aggression, 161 *et seq.*
  on the lead, 168

Agility competitions, 156–157

Alsatian (see German Shepherd Dog)

Anal glands, 191

Barking, 93–96

Bathing, 187–188

Bed (see also First night) 38, 39

Behaviour, 91 *et seq.*
  , inconsistent, 73–74, 170
  , unacceptable, 71–72, 99, 161 *et seq.*

Bichon Frise, 211–213

Bitch, owning a, 17

Boarding kennels, 22

Border Collies, 14, 213–215

Boundaries, 71

Boxer, 215–217

Breeders, registered, 25–26

Breeding,177–180
  terms, 26

Breeds: Sporting, 243

Buying from
  advertisements, 27–28
  breeders, 25–26
  friend or family, 27
  pet shops, 26–27
  puppy farms, 28
  rescue centres, 29–30

Calling name, 134–135

Castration, 176–177

Cataracts, 193

Chemicals, 48

Chewing, 99–101

Children and dogs, 19–21

Choke chain (see Training chains)

Collars and leads (see also Law)
  for adult dogs, 43–44
  for formal training, 44 *et seq.*
  for puppies, 43
  , how to use, 107–108

Conjunctivitis, 193

Cost of ownership, 23–24

Crossbreed, 15, 221–222

Cystitis, 191–192

Dalmatian, 222–224

Dangerous Dogs Act,
200–201
Dangers around home,
47–48, 69
Diarrhoea, 192
Diet, incorrect, 174
, natural, 57 *et seq.*, 105
Digging pit, 48
Down, stay, 121–124
Ear infections, 192
Eclampsia, 193
Entropion, 193
Examining, 72–73, 84–85
Exercise, 16–17, 188–189
, lack of, 100
Faeces, eating, 105
, owner picking up, 200
, rolling in, 105–106
Feeding (see also
Diet/Food) 47, 57 *et
seq.*, 74–75, 76
Fences, 48
First-aid, 198
First night, 51
Fleas, 21, 54, 184–185
Food (see also Diet)
, possessiveness with,
69–70
Gastric dilation (see
Torsion)
German Shepherd Dog,
224–227
Golden Retriever,
227–230
Great Dane, 230–231
Grooming, 19, 72, 84–85,
187
Gundogs, 13, 244–245
Head collar, 44, 153

Heatstroke, 193–195
Heel (see also Lead,
walking on the)
, return to, 149–153
Holidays, 22–23
Hounds, 13, 243–244
House-training, 51, 53,
72, 77–83
Howling, 100–101
Identity discs, 24, 43–44,
46, 55, 199
, temporary, 23
Indoor kennels for
puppies, 39–41
for adult dogs, 42
Inoculations, 181–182
Jumping up, 91–93
Kennel Club, 25, 51, 251
cough, 195
, indoor, 39–42
Labrador, 234–235
Law, your dog and the,
107, 141, 181, 199 *et
seq.*
Lead (see also Collars
and leads)
, walking on the,
140–153, 199–200
, lagging when,
148–149
Leather collars, 45–46
Leaving adult dogs, 86–88
puppies, 85–86
Lice, 186
Lying down, 117–121
Male dog, owning a, 17
Microchipping, 24, 54–55,
199
Mongrel, 15

Mounting, 104
Mouthing and biting,
    97–99
Name (see also Calling
    name)
    , choice of, 37
    for adult dog, new, 38
Natural feeding (see Diet,
    natural)
Non-sporting dogs, 13,
    246–247
Obedience competitions,
    154–155
Pastoral dogs, 13, 14,
    247–248
Pedigree, 13–15, 50
Pet Travel Scheme, 22,
    181, 201–203
Possessiveness (see also
    Food) 169, 207
    towards people, 172
Puppies (see also
    House-training) 18
    , choosing, 31–35
    , collecting, 35–36, 50,
    171–172
Puppy parties, 88–89
Pyometra, 195–196
Quarantine, 181, 200, 203
Rabies, 191
Rank structuring, 74–77
Recall, 133–139
Rescue dog, 18
Retrieving, 102, 139–140
Ringworm, 190, 196
Routine, 53, 72–73, 77
Sarcoptic mange, 190, 196
Season, 175, 176
Second dog, 207 et seq.

Setter (Irish or Red),
    231–233
Settle, 124–125
Skin conditions, 196
Showing, 157–160
Shows, 154, 158–159
Sitting and staying,
    114–117
    on command,109–114
Size, 16–17
Sleep, putting to, 205–206
Sleeping (see Bed)
Slip collars, rope and
    nylon, 45
Snake bites, 186–187
Socialising (see also
    Puppy parties) 167,
    172
Sounds, accustoming to,
    83–84
Spaniel, Cavalier King
    Charles, 217–219
    , Cocker, 219–221
    , English Springer,
    235–237
    , Welsh, 238–239
Spaying, 85, 175–176
Sporting dogs, 13,
    243–246
Stand, 129–133
Steady (see Lead, walking
    on the)
Stealing, 99, 101–102,
    162–163
Stings, 185–186
Swimming, 188
Teeth, 59, 189–190
    , cleaning, 85, 189–190
Teething, 101

Temperament, 14–15, 18,
    31–32, 33, 34, 173
  and diet, 59
  and castration, 176–177
  of stud dogs, 178
Terriers, 13, 245–246
Ticks, 186, 203
Torsion, 196–197
Toy dogs, 249–250
Toys, 42–43, 77
Training (see also
    House-training)
    10–11, 52–53, 55–56,
    73–74, 88–90, 107 *et
    seq*.
  , advanced, 154 *et seq*.
  chains, 44–45
  clubs, 89–90
  collar, double action,
    46–47

, incorrect basic,
    167–170
Transfer of ownership
    form, 51
Travel sickness, 102–103
Utility dogs, 13, 248–249
Vaccinations, 53
Veterinary surgeon,
    choosing a, 49
  , visiting the, 53–54
Visitors, 55–56
Visual signals, 108–109
Voice, tones of, 108–109
Vomiting, 197
Wait, 125–127
West Highland White,
    239–241
Working dogs, 13
  trials, 156
Worming, 53, 66, 182–184
Yorkshire Terrier, 241–242